TOBY MILDON

INCLUSIVE GROWTH

Future-proof your business by creating a diverse workplace

RETHINK PRESS

First published in Great Britain in 2020 by Rethink Press
(www.rethinkpress.com)

Cover image © Shutterstock | Vectoraart

Contents

Introduction

I first became involved in diversity and inclusion when I was working for the BBC as a project manager on the redevelopment of the BBC News website, the development of the iPlayer Radio app (now BBC Sounds) and various digital accessibility projects. The Chief Operating Officer (COO) of Design and Engineering was concerned about the gender imbalance within the technology division of the BBC. Being a techie part of the Corporation, we had more men than women in contrast to the approximate 50:50 ratio in the rest of the BBC. The COO had formulated an action plan and needed a project manager to implement it. I took on the role and quickly discovered how passionate I was about diversity and inclusion. It soon became my full-time role. It is testament to the BBC that the divisional directors understood the importance of diversity and inclusion to the division. Eventually, I moved into a central Centre of Expertise team reporting to a recently appointed Head of Diversity and Inclusion within the HR department, responsible for the whole of the BBC and not just technology. This new development raised the question for me about where diversity and inclusion should sit within the organisation. Prior to this I was embedded as a specialist within the technology division, reporting to a Chief Operating Officer with access to the right people, well-networked in the area and with a dedicated budget. Yet being in HR meant I could take on a much bigger portfolio. Before long, I was responsible for Radio and all the BBC's corporate services like finance, legal, workplace buildings, procurement and HR.

I learnt several clear lessons in this role, and in my subsequent position at a large consultancy firm in a similar role. Firstly, the importance of the full support of the Chief Executive in implementing the diversity and inclusion strategy. This endorsement meant that the organisation took notice and got behind the strategy. Secondly, the backing of the senior leadership team. Again, this raised the profile of the strategy and resulted in every department becoming involved in the implementation. And finally, the location of the diversity and inclusion manager within the organisation and their degree of access to senior leaders. I explore all three of these factors in this book as having them in place right from the start of implementation is vital. Otherwise, you may find yourself frustrated by the lack of impact you're making in changing your organisation into a more diverse and inclusive one. You may even be experiencing this frustration right now.

Why I wrote this book

As a Diversity and Inclusion Manager, I became frustrated at the lack of impact I felt I could personally make. The speed of change was slow and when I talked to other Diversity and Inclusion Managers, they were experiencing the same issues as me, such as:

- Not enough time to do the job

- Not adequately resourced in terms of people and budget

- Lacking senior level engagement (senior leaders who didn't 'walk the talk')

- Not enough attention being paid to the culture of the organisation

- Thinking that suggests diversity begins and ends with women. Or organisations being #Diverseish by implementing change for women this year, planning for ethnicity next quarter, considering LGBT+ for the next financial year and stating that disability is not a priority for the organisation. I recommend you find out more about #Diverseish by visiting their website at www.thevaluable500 .com.

- A lack of awareness of the whole spectrum of diversity that can reside in one individual. Or intersectionality, as we call it in the trade. For example, I'm a man, gay, disabled and sarcastic.

- Wasting time filling in award entries that don't really change the inclusivity or the lived experience of employees day-to-day.

This realisation led me to set up my own diversity and inclusion consultancy. I wanted to enable organisations to implement diversity and inclusion properly and in a sustainable way. Instead of trying to fix individuals and implement programmatic short-term interventions, I wanted organisations to take an intersectional, human-centred approach that is long-lasting and can future-proof the organisation.

That's why I wrote this book. I passionately want change to happen quicker and I want those who are responsible for diversity and inclusion to make a bigger impact, a bigger difference to their workplace and their industry. Our workplaces are important for society and it frustrates me that when I talk to younger disabled people, I discover that they are experiencing similar challenges finding meaningful work to those I faced when I entered the workforce twenty years ago. They still come up against unconscious biases and prejudice and are told what they can't do and not recognised for their innate talents. Work gives all of us structure and purpose. It plays an essential role in our lives, our mental health, our economic standing, and our ability to contribute to improving the world. I don't want future generations to face the same struggles I have had to deal with.

This passion led me to set up my own business to help support organisations implement diversity and inclusion more effectively. From my experience I could see that there were clear steps to take that would result in sea-change, a new way of thinking that would address the problems Diversity and Inclusion Managers were facing. The Inclusive Growth System, structured around the seven 'C's which make an organisation a great place to work, is the result of my research into the best practice for implementing diversity and inclusion in an organisation. This book will guide you through each step so that you can make the changes that mean your organisation will develop an exceptional reputation for being an inclusive workplace.

The Inclusive Growth System

At the centre of every industry is an organisation that is renowned as a great place to work. You probably know these organisations because they:

- easily attract talent

- can retain their people and keep them happy

- innovate at a high pace

- reach new markets and engage with their customers

- are publicly recognised as a great place to work

These positives all stem from inclusive growth. To achieve inclusive growth, you need to deploy these seven best practices:

- **Clarity**: why diversity and inclusion is important to the organisation, what kind of language gains traction, how the CEO and leadership will take responsibility and ownership for building an inclusive culture.

- **Culture**: the importance of culture over tactics and how organisations can define and create their inclusive culture.

- **Change**: the importance of treating diversity and inclusion like any other important change programme within the organisation.

- **Colleague Experience and Design**: how to take design-thinking and human-centered design to re-engineer systems and processes to be more inclusive. This is the core of the model and helps 'hardwire' inclusion into your organisation.

- **Cyber**: leveraging the power of technology, for instance, artificial intelligence, to create inclusive recruitment processes.

- **Collaboration**: working with others in the industry, from strategic partners to customers, in order to create inclusive organisations.

- **Celebrate**: communicate inclusion successes and best practices effectively across the industry, demonstrating how inclusive workplaces are to the public and to prospective employees. Become an employer of choice.

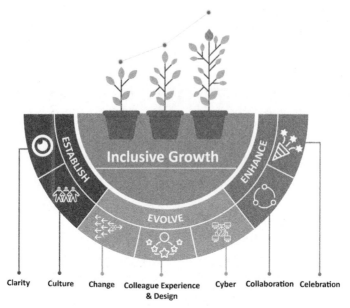

The Inclusive Growth System

Each chapter in this book will cover each of the seven C's and give you detailed information on how you can implement each one in an effective and sustainable way.

Who is this book for?

If you are a CEO, HR Director or a Diversity and Inclusion Manager who feels exasperated at the slow pace of change in diversity and inclusion in your organisation or are concerned that it is simply a box-ticking exercise, then I would encourage you to read this book from beginning to end. Or perhaps you are just starting to think about the importance of diversity and inclusion to your organisation and need a framework or structure to help you implement it. You might be feeling overwhelmed by everything that you could or should be doing and need some clarity on how to proceed.

It is my hope that you will find that the Inclusive Growth System will give you a new way of thinking and that you will find solutions, techniques and strategies to enable you to begin to make changes that will have a greater impact for all of the employees in your organisation.

How to use this book

Put simply, work from left to right. Take one step at a time and learn how each of the seven 'C's builds on the one before. Identify which areas are implemented well in your organisations and which need improvement.

As part of my research for writing this book, I interviewed leaders in business, HR, diversity and inclusion in key organisations around the UK. These interviews are included as Case Studies at the end of each chapter and will add to your learning by demonstrating how these organisations have implemented their diversity and inclusion strategies effectively.

Finally, I have included a section for reflection at the end of each chapter – questions that, I hope, will broaden your thinking about how diversity and inclusion might be better implemented within your own organisation.

I see this system as a vehicle for growth for the organisation. Because of this, when you have finished reading this book, I urge you to give a copy to your Chief Executive and then have a conversation with them about how diversity and inclusion can be improved in your organisation. Diversity and inclusion is there to help an organisation grow, but some organisations 'do' diversity and inclusion only because they believe that it's the right thing to do. But diversity and inclusion is proved to generate better innovation, foster better decision-making and result in better financial performance. There is now statistical evidence that demonstrates that this is not just the right thing to do, it is commercially imperative to an organisation. We will go on to look at this evidence in Chapter 1.

ONE

Clarity

The importance of diversity and inclusion in organisations

There is a misunderstanding in many organisations about what is meant by diversity. Many organisations think that diversity begins and ends with gender, promoting a particular cause such as increasing the number of women in leadership roles. But diversity includes everybody. It is about what makes us unique.

When we talk about diversity, we could look at it from the Equality Act (2010)[1] perspective. It lists nine protected characteristics:

---

1   Equality Act (2010), www.legislation.gov.uk/ukpga/2010/15
    /contents

- age

- disability

- gender reassignment

- marriage and civil partnership

- pregnancy and maternity

- race

- religion or belief

- sex

- sexual orientation

However, we need to move beyond the Equality Act. I like to think about diversity as an iceberg. Above the waterline is 10% of the iceberg, including the nine 'protected' characteristics and any other visible characteristics. But so much lies beneath the waterline that makes us different too, such as whether you are an introvert or extrovert, whether you had a private or public education, whether you grew up in a military family and moved around, whether you are a parent or not, or whether you have an invisible disability such as dyslexia. This is how I define diversity. When it comes to the diversity and inclusion debate, we need to talk a lot more about inclusion. Inclusion can be defined as the action, practice, or policy of including any person in an activity, system, organization, or process. The key to our understanding of inclusion in the diversity context is that the person is included irrespective of aspects of their identity, such as race, gender, religion, age, or ability. Our focus should be on creating more inclusive workplaces that welcome everybody and allow all employees to thrive within the organisation.

The importance of diversity and inclusion in an organisation can be broken down into at least three cases:

- business case

- employee case

- customer case

Taking the business case first, organisations that are more diverse perform better. The McKinsey Report (2018) 'Delivering Through Diversity'[2] talks about the business case for diversity and includes many useful statistics, for example: 'Companies in the top-quartile for gender diversity on their executive teams were 21% more likely to have above-average profitability than companies in the fourth quartile.

---

2   Hunt, V, Prince, S, Dixon-Fyle, S, Yee, L (Jan 2018) 'Delivering through Diversity' Report. McKinsey & Company, p8, www .mckinsey.com/business-functions/organization/our-insights /delivering-through-diversity

For ethnic/cultural diversity, top-quartile companies were 33% more likely to outperform on profitability.' Not only that, but greater diversity means more innovation and better problem-solving.

The employee case is based on having an inclusive workplace. If an organisation has inclusivity across the whole company, it is easier to attract talent and retain people because employee satisfaction is higher. Plus, the amount of creativity increases along with the ability to solve problems.

Finally, the customer case. A diverse workforce can relate better to a diverse customer base. Organisations often find that their customer base is a lot more diverse than the people they employ. It is important to recognise that they need to employ a workforce that mirrors the diversity of their customers. They will be better able to anticipate customers' needs, innovate more, build better rapport, improve customer satisfaction and resolve customer complaints more effectively.

Ultimately, the more inclusive an organisation is, the more it will grow. This is the key point of my book. An organisation that is more inclusive should expect to grow in each of these three areas – business, employee and customer. Growth will mean different things to different organisations. A non-profit-making organisation might want to see growth in donations or reputation. A commercial company will want to grow its profitability. Consequently, diversity and inclusion needs to underpin whatever 'growth' means to an organisation. I believe that the diversity dividend – the benefit of a diverse workforce and an inclusive culture – results in an organisation that is both resilient and more able to grow. We need to increase the diversity dividend and encourage organisations to link the business case for diversity to the growth of the organisation, whatever growth means for them.

Aligning diversity and inclusion with vision, mission and values

Many organisations do not position diversity and inclusion strategically. They think short term and tactically. I've already mentioned the importance of connecting diversity and inclusion to growth, but it is also important to align it with the organisation's vision, mission and values. To do this an organisation needs to understand how a diverse workforce and an inclusive culture enables it to achieve its vision and mission.

Take, as an example, the BBC's vision to be the most creative organisation in the world. As I've said, a more diverse workforce increases creativity and innovation. Consequently, for the BBC, having a more diverse workforce should equal greater imagination and new ideas to enable it to become the most creative organisation in the world. This demonstrates the alignment needed between diversity and inclusion and vision. An example of values, again from the BBC, is 'We are one BBC. Great things happen when we work together.' There is perfect alignment between this value and inclusion, emphasising the BBC's belief that if they are more inclusive, they can work better together, and so great things can happen. This perfect alignment is something all organisations should strive for. Similarly, diversity and inclusion has to align with the organisation's mission. Of course, it is arguable whether employees actually know their organisation's values and mission. When I run strategy workshops with organisations, I do an exercise about aligning diversity and inclusion with their vision, mission and values. It is interesting to find that many people struggle to remember what their organisational values are. However, many organisations have a value that is closely aligned to diversity and inclusion which you can usually find in their recruitment materials, on their website and in their on-boarding collateral for new employees.

Some organisations will even frame these values on office walls or inscribe them on the back of ID badges. Better still, they find ways of enabling their employees to live the organisational values day in, day out, and lead by example.

Choosing the right language

There is diversity fatigue in organisations these days. People are getting tired of hearing about it. In fact, the more we talk about diversity, the more it feels like it is creating divisions in organisations, even among groups that would consider themselves less included. This is because organisations are not talking about the whole spectrum of diversity. Often, it's just gender and ethnicity. They don't do much on LGBT+ or certainly, disability, which is often at the bottom of the hierarchy. This is a missed trick. If organisations led with disability, they would find that they solve a lot of issues for many other employees. But they are often afraid to go there. Diversity fatigue is occurring because of this hierarchical attitude. People feel left out because diversity seems to be all about gender: whether it be putting women in leadership roles or simply increasing numbers across the rest of the organisation. I think this is dangerous, particularly

in relation to straight, white men. Rather than feeling
ostracised and threatened, they need to be part
of the solution and engaged in the conversation.
Campaigns such as the 'Me Too' Movement have
also made men wary about mentoring women.

This means we have to be thoughtful about the
language we use. 'Diversity' and 'inclusion' are not
helpful words in themselves. We are all diverse –
remember the iceberg, and the many hidden
characteristics that can exist in one person. We have
to respect and value difference. But organisations
need to think about the language they use and how
it sounds to their workforce. Deloitte is an example
of an organisation that does not talk about *diversity*
and inclusion. They talk about *respect* and inclusion.
This is the culture they want to promote, and they
would rather focus on the behaviour of respect
and the value of inclusion. This language has been
well received in the organisation. It is evident in all
their internal communications. It is something that
employees talk easily and openly about. If other
organisations can get their employees to talk this
way about diversity and inclusion, or whatever
words they choose to use, it is a good place to be.

Other organisations often refer to diversity and
'belonging'. Some even put inclusion before diversity
because they want to focus on this area first. It

demonstrates how important it is for organisations to play around with the language and link it to their values. BBC employees are very clear about the values of their company. 'We are one BBC' is the one I remember best from my time there. Organisations should think carefully about the language they use, find a value that resonates with employees, link this to diversity and inclusion and ensure it is embraced across the board.

How exclusion occurs within the workplace

There are many causes for exclusion in the workplace. The ones I want to focus on are:

- **Micro-aggressions and micro-inequities**

- **Unconscious bias**

- **Norms**

- **Privilege**

- **Fear, ignorance and lack of understanding**

Micro-aggressions and micro-inequities

I prefer to talk about micro-inequities rather than micro-aggressions. Micro-inequities are small slights of behaviour that demean you or put you down. It might be because of your gender, ethnicity or a visible disability. Have you ever been in a meeting and put forward an idea which gets ignored, but the person sitting next to you gets credit for the same idea? That's micro-inequity. Women experience this frequently. People from ethnic minority backgrounds experience micro-inequities when they are constantly addressed by the wrong name. As a wheelchair user, I frequently get comments such as, 'How fast can you go in that thing?' or 'Don't run over my toes'. These small slights of behaviour have a compound effect, bringing you down and chipping away at your confidence. Many people are unaware of these micro-inequities. They don't even realise that they are committing them. And they are certainly oblivious to their effects.

Unconscious bias

There are many academic definitions of unconscious bias, but I prefer that of Verna Myers. She is currently Vice President of Inclusion Strategy at Netflix. A

Harvard-trained lawyer in the US, she has done a lot of work around diversity and inclusion. In one of her TED talks she says that unconscious bias is the stories we make up about people before we get to know them. There are, in fact, about 140 different types of cognitive bias (and counting). In a 2019 blog post by Chris Weller of the Neuroleadership Institute, he discusses the model of five biases, called the **SEEDS** model:[3]

- Similarity bias

- Experience bias

- Expedience bias

- Distance bias

- Safety bias

With **Similarity bias**, we tend to hire in our own image. I worked with an HR director who once said, 'I often thought that opposites attract, but now I know that birds of a feather flock together.' This is because we have our own biases. It's human nature. It is partly the way our brains are wired and partly social conditioning through the messages we

---

3   Weller, C (Apr 2019) 'The 5 Biggest Biases that Affect Decision-Making', https://neuroleadership.com/your-brain-at-work/seeds-model-biases-affect-decision-making

have received from people in power, politics, media, parenting and education.

We can do something about unconscious bias by increasing awareness. But we need to do more, because unconscious bias training doesn't work on its own. It requires action. You can do the training and then take the Harvard Implicit Association Test, devised by Anthony Greenwald, Debbie McGhee and Jordan Schwartz in 1998 to find out whether you're biased towards particular groups of people.[4]

I am moderately biased against disabled people apparently. This is ironic given that I was born with a neuromuscular disability, have a disabled brother and many disabled friends and colleagues. Now that I am aware of it, are there going to be unintended consequences the next time I am faced with a disabled person and I have to make a decision that could affect them? Will I fight to give them a job or promote them? Am I going to take corrective action? Am I going to be a bit more lenient on them or not? What is important is understanding bias in the decisions that we make.

---

4   Greenwald, AG, McGhee, DE, Schwartz, Jordan, JLK (1998) 'Measuring Individual Differences in Implicit Cognition: The Implicit Association Test', *Journal of Personality and Social Psychology*, 74(6), pp1464–1480

I use a simple formula called 'If this, then that'. When I go to a meeting – a creative meeting, an ideas generation meeting – I might take my **Experience bias** with me and shoot down all the ideas because I believe we've tried them all before. This attitude is based on my prior experience. But if I adopt the 'If this, then that' strategy, whenever I hear an idea I'm not sure about, I say to myself, 'IF I hear a new idea THEN I'll say "Yes, and…" rather than, "No, but…".' Instead of instantly closing down the idea, it leaves it open for further discussion.

Another method to help with bias is reverse mentoring. Normal mentoring is where a senior, more experienced person mentors the more junior, inexperienced person. In reverse mentoring, the senior person's world can be opened up by being mentored by somebody who is younger and perhaps from a different background. Particularly if they can teach them a skill that they don't possess.

There are three categories in reverse mentoring:

1. **Lean back** – where you educate yourself by watching a TED talk or a YouTube video about something you wouldn't normally watch, eg someone from an ethnic minority background

talking about what challenges they may face at work.

2. **Lean forward** – means networking and engaging with people. My favourite tool for this is Meetup.com, where you find lots of networking groups. For example, you could go to an LGBT+ Professionals Network Group to network with new people. Many organisations have diversity networks and employee resource groups which you can go along to.

3. **Step in** – find a mentor. Find somebody in a neighbouring team and invite them out to a local coffee shop to understand what it's like for them to work in your organisation. Ideally, you should spot a talent or skill they can teach you.

Norms

These are exclusive unwritten rules. Norms are useful in companies because they help organise us. In most organisations people are expected to turn up to meetings on time and stick to deadlines. These are norms that you might want to preserve. But there are some norms in businesses that you might want to push back on, like the fact that airline pilots are usually men. Or that it is assumed that women take on the caring roles, and men in the organisation are not seen as active parents or carers. This norm can cause exclusion, contribute to your gender pay gap and should be challenged.

Privilege

Firstly, privilege is nobody's fault. A lot of us experience privilege at different times of our lives. It is purely the result of the circumstances that we are born into. According to the *Cambridge Dictionary*, privilege is 'an advantage that only one person or group of people has'. France Winddance Twine in *Geographies of Privilege* (2013)[5] states that 'these groups can be advantaged based on age, education level, disability, ethnic or racial category, gender, gender identity, sexual orientation, religion, and social class. It is generally considered to be a theoretical concept used in a variety of subjects and often linked to social inequality. Privilege is also linked to social and cultural forms of power.'

Privilege means that some people have a head start in life. Everyone has the ability to run the same race, but some people can set out faster from the start line. This is why I think it is essential to understand the effects of privilege. We need to support each other,

---

5   Twine, France Winddance (2013) *Geographies of Privilege*, Routledge, pp8–10

to help those who are not as advantaged as us and make sure they are offered the same opportunities.

Fear, ignorance and lack of understanding

Ignorance is not always deliberate. Sometimes we are ignorant about the effects of our behaviour, or what's right and wrong, and have a lack of understanding or empathy of other people's situations. In one of my first jobs after university I was at a client's office. It was an old 1940s telephone exchange (and not the most wheelchair-accessible building in London). The Health and Safety manager told me to leave the building. He said I was a fire risk. I decided to go back to the office another day. It just so happened that the Health and Safety manager chose the same day for another visit. I ended up in tears in the disabled toilet. As the employee I felt very let down. It was one of the reasons why I decided to leave that employer.

Another incident happened recently when I started a new job. I was looking forward to the Christmas party because the whole department was going, and I wanted to network and meet people from outside my immediate team. When the invitation was emailed, it turned out that the chosen venue was wheelchair inaccessible. It was in an old building. I would have to go down a flight of stairs, and there was no way I could get in. The venue offered to carry me down the stairs in my heavy electric wheelchair, but that was undignified and unsafe. They didn't have a disabled toilet either. Even if I could get into the venue, I wouldn't have been able to go to the toilet. So, I couldn't go to the party and I felt excluded. This was due to ignorance and a lack of understanding. The people organising the event did not put any thought into the fact that the venue should have been wheelchair accessible to accommodate the whole team.

However, there is also a lot of fear about saying or doing the wrong thing. What I find is that people are afraid of saying or doing the wrong thing in case it causes offence or they embarrass themselves. They avoid interacting with people or make assumptions about what they need or don't need or can or can't do. But it's important to face this head on. We need to have braver conversations, be more curious, and open to making mistakes in the knowledge that we are doing it in a supportive and well-intentioned way.

Appreciating the employee experience

Every organisation needs to get an understanding and appreciation of their employees' experience. There are several ways to do this. The first is to undertake an employee experience exercise and survey your employees to find out what their day-to-day work is like. But be aware that if you do this exercise, you need to be able to dissect or cut the data by different diversity cohorts. At the bare minimum, the survey should align with the nine protected characteristics of the Equality Act. You want to find out what the employee experience is like for men compared to women, for employees from an ethnic minority background compared to those who are not, for disabled employees compared to non-disabled employees, for LGBT+ compared to non-LGBT+ employees. It is essential to understand what makes your employees tick – what annoys them, what makes them happy, their fears, anxieties and frustrations. How does an employee feel at a particular point in their work lifecycle? What is it like as a new employee or for somebody who has been there for a long time? Or for somebody who is trying for promotion? What is it like for a first-time parent, or for an employee who has just been diagnosed with a disability or long-term health condition? If you break down the employee lifecycle in this way, you will end up with a matrix of valuable information.

An organisation can consider several ways of collecting this information.

Annual engagement surveys

Most organisations carry out an annual engagement survey. A very simple solution is to include a diversity questionnaire in this exercise. You can extract the diversity data from your annual engagement survey, rather than carrying out a separate diversity and inclusion survey. I find that you get better data from this approach because the annual engagement survey is usually anonymous. It helps to use a trusted third party to conduct your survey, as it gives your employees confidence that the data will be objectively handled and analysed.

Pulse surveys

Many organisations use pulse surveys, randomly picking a group of employees to survey every quarter. In this type of survey, they might select 25% of their employees in quarter one and another 25% in quarter two, and so on. Questions are tweaked and adapted throughout the year.

Focus groups

Conducting focus groups with employees often provides a wide range of information about staff's personal and group feelings. A focus group is also a cost-effective way of capturing useful data from several employees at the same time. It also allows them to bounce thoughts and ideas off each other.

Exit interviews

Many organisations do not conduct exit interviews properly. As they are not mandatory, many employees choose not to have one. But you can get good insights from exit interviews. An exit interview can provide a 360-degree feedback system where the employee can give feedback on their line manager. The exit interview can be aligned with organisational values, with targeted questions on how the manager measures up to them.

Whistleblowing and ethics hotline

Many organisations have a whistleblowing and ethics hotline where employees can report issues.

These include bullying and harassment, breaking the code of ethics, or concerns around criminal activity such as money laundering. Employees have confidence in reporting issues because it is anonymous and usually managed through a trusted third party. This third party can usually report high-level (or 'noteworthy') diversity and inclusion problems back to your organisation.

Employee assistance programmes

These programmes offer staff free counselling, advice and support through third-party providers. These providers can offer high-level feedback on the trends and themes they hear from staff.

Quantitative data

A great amount of data is available from HR management information systems: attrition and retention statistics, the amount of time that people spend at different grades, etc, as well as staff diversity. This means you can see if employees from an ethnic minority background stay at a particular grade longer than average, and ask the question- 'Why are they not progressing as fast as other people in the organisation?'

Performance Management

Many organisations use a 3 × 3 grid or bell curve to plot employee performance. If you can dissect this data by different diversity cohorts, you might find that there is rarely a disabled person in the high-performing box. Again, it is an opportunity to ask why these employees don't reach this quadrant of the performance management box.

Create a strategy everyone understands

Once data has been collected, this information can be used to formulate a diversity strategy. It is vital that organisations think 'intersectional' rather than 'silo' and do not simply create a strategy for women, another for ethnicity, another for disability and another for LGBT+. We are all intersectional beings. I am disabled, male, white and gay myself. By thinking intersectionally, you can create efficiency. Let's take the issue of toilets. You don't have to have traditionally separate male, female and disabled toilets. When you think intersectionally, you can have gender-neutral toilets. Or simply accessible toilets. You might even want to think about toilets for guide dogs for any blind employees. The key is having one conversation about toilets rather than separating it into silos.

An organisation's strategy ideally fits on one page so that everyone understands it and stays fully engaged. A key component is how organisations take targeted action to change their culture. Andrew Cave's article (2017) on Forbes website quotes the management consultant Peter Drucker: 'Culture eats strategy for breakfast.'[6]

To shape your strategy, think about how your organisation is positioned. Is it expanding? If it is, do you need to focus your efforts on attracting and recruiting talent and getting diversity through the door? If you're not recruiting, maybe your strategy should focus on retaining employees and creating a place where people feel they belong.

Organisations often treat diversity in a superficial way. Perhaps they do something on International Women's Day, or in Black History Month, or they sponsor the annual Pride festival in their city. While this does raise awareness and makes people feel more confident, it is no substitute for addressing

6   Cave, A (Nov 2017) 'Culture Eats Strategy for Breakfast. So What's for Lunch?', www.forbes.com/sites/andrewcave/2017/11/09/culture -eats-strategy-for-breakfast-so-whats-for-lunch

how the organisation embraces diversity within its day-to-day operations. For instance, how efficient and effective is its 'reasonable adjustments' process? Are disabled staff being let down by not getting the adjustments they require in a timely manner? Does the organisation provide flexible or agile working, so that working parents, employees with elderly parents to care for, or people with fluctuating health conditions can balance their life/work commitments appropriately? How are work assignments allocated? Are they allocated in a fair way or by tapping someone on the shoulder? This approach is prone to unconscious bias. Often interesting projects are given to people who are considered a safe pair of hands. This is biased against someone else who might need that career-defining moment but hasn't yet been given the opportunity.

Your strategy should focus on at least three key areas:

- What you do to attract and recruit greater diversity into your organisation

- What you do to retain and develop people within your organisation

- What you do to create a more inclusive culture

Creating the dashboard

Once you have your strategy, you need to create
a dashboard to enable the organisation to monitor
whether it is becoming more inclusive and if its
diversity is improving. Organisations should reflect
the diversity of the communities in which they
operate and which they serve. An organisation
based in London is different to an organisation
based in Exeter because the diversity make-up of the
two cities is quite different. The dashboard reports
whether the organisation is successfully moving
towards a diverse workforce that reflects its customer
base and available talent pool.

Set goals to keep your focus. Monitor progress and
trends. If you can see from your dashboard that
attrition is worsening over time for a particular
characteristic or group of people, the organisation
needs to investigate. Intervention will be required to
turn this situation around.

The dashboard reflects the different journeys or
funnels people move through. If you look at the
recruitment funnel, what is the diversity like
at different stages of recruitment? How many
applications are received? How many of those get
a screening call? How many get a first interview or

are called back for a second interview? How many of those get a job offer? How many candidates accept or reject those offers? Diversity should be monitored at each stage of the funnel. The dashboard should also show data for anyone who is promoted or leaves the organisation.

Using this information, the organisation can set targets to enhance diversity and inclusion. Targets are aspirational goals. Quotas tend to be mandated and carry some sort of penalty. Somebody once said that what gets measured, gets done. It is essential that organisations, when considering the diversity of their workforce, can measure data and set goals. This demonstrates whether they are making progress or not.

CASE STUDY: DON'T CONFUSE ALTRUISM AND BUSINESS

Peter Cheese is the Chief Executive of the Chartered Institute of Personnel and Development (CIPD), a role he's had for over seven years. The Institute began over one hundred years ago, starting as the Welfare Workers' Association. Now the professional body for HR and People Development, it represents nearly 160,000 members and has offices in Dubai, Dublin, London and Singapore.

A large part of the mission is to grow, support and professionalise HR. To this end, CIPD offers qualification frameworks at all levels, and training in core areas of HR and learning and development. Training needs are growing as the profession steps up and holds itself to account. CIPD also acts as the voice of HR, contributing to policy development, research and media. This influencing presence flows back into membership building professional confidence.

'How long have we been talking about diversity and inclusion?'

This frustrates Peter. He believes organisations are still struggling. On a positive note, he says diversity and inclusion is talked about more and taken seriously. To accelerate progress, he insists it's imperative that diversity and inclusion is anchored strategically. Organisations should be clear why it is important to the business. He admits shifting a legacy of certain thinking, mindsets and cultures is not easy to do, which is why it takes time.

Strategic importance of diversity and inclusion

If diversity and inclusion isn't part of the strategic agenda, it can be seen as just being politically correct, or a trendy compliance box to be ticked. Peter is adamant that diversity and inclusion is profoundly central to sustainable business. Whether it's strategic workforce planning, authentically reflecting the customer base, building talent supply lines, or creating a responsive and responsible business in touch with their communities, adaptive organisations are supported by diversity.

Shifting Cultures

Firstly, recognise the issues that need dealing with. Next, ask, 'What are we measuring?' What gets measured gets done. The challenge is to create a deeper understanding of diversity, a subject not always easy to understand because not all diversity is visible. Understand that people develop coping mechanisms to shield some of those differences because they have learned that organisations want certain types of people.

Set goals and targets. Ask 'How will we know when we are achieving the target?' Speak openly about effecting change through metrics. Root interventions in the psychology and behavioural science evidence base. Let people know why data is being collected. Approach the task with sensitivity because people don't like being put in categories. Be transparent about how engaging with the data will ultimately benefit individuals.

Leaders need to walk the talk. Shift the language from diversity to inclusion, where common things can be done to support everyone. This helps small and medium-sized enterprises, where there aren't as many resources. Create a culture where people can speak truth to power. Establish networks for sharing personal experiences. Offer flexible working.

These things build the foundations and should be the norm. Interventions can then be specifically targeted and the superficial checklist approach to diversity and inclusion avoided. This approach in parallel with a strategic narrative helps avoid feelings of tokenism.

Advice to HR Directors

Don't confuse altruism and business. Establish why diversity and inclusion is strategically important to the business. You might want to consider workforce planning in times of high employment for instance and educate business leaders. The HR voice hasn't always been good at articulating the strategic context of diversity and inclusion through business language. Bring the evidence and numbers into these conversations: the make-up of the workforce, skills shortfalls, homogenous teams unreflective of the customer base, recruitment and retention issues for diverse talent.

Peter is adamant. 'HR Directors need to make an evidence-based case to a sceptical CEO as to why this is strategically important. You can't wing it. Get the evidence. With it, you can tell a compelling story.'

He concludes 'Customers are diverse, and a workforce needs to reflect that. Myopic thinking allows inherent biases to get in the way of what we should have been doing all along.'

REFLECTION

Take a few moments to answer the following questions:

1. How closely aligned is your diversity and inclusion plan with the organisation's strategy, vision, mission and values?

2. How will diversity and inclusion enable your organisation to grow?

3. How are you measuring progress against your goals?

4. How are you mining data to better understand the employee experience?

5. How intersectional are your strategy and action plans, if you have them?

In the next chapter we cover the all-important topic of culture in an organisation and how culture impacts on diversity and inclusion. I describe easy steps to take to create an inclusive culture within your organisation.

TWO

Culture

Why is culture so important?

When organisations create the right culture, employee engagement and retention go up. This leads to growth for the organisation. Researchers have found that the most profitable organisations are not actually the most profit-focused. They are the most people-focused. Rachael Down in her article (2019)[1] 'What is company culture and why is it important?' wrote, 'Contrary to what some HR specialists are led to believe, studies demonstrate that the most profitable companies are not actually the most profit-focused. Through switching their target from profit to purpose, employees and

---

1   Down, R (Feb 2019) 'What is Company Culture and Why is it Important?', www.breathehr.com/blog/what-is-company-culture-and-why-is-it-important

employers alike gain greater role-fulfilment, which in turn increases productivity, efficiency and quality results.'

Organisations that prioritise profit over people find that the mental and physical wellbeing of employees drops, employee retention falls and engagement scores of employees dip as well. Organisations should not underestimate the power of online platforms and the impact of social media. This environment makes it even more important to get the culture right for your employees. The recent BBC controversy over the gender pay gap and Uber's 'toxic' culture featured widely on social media. Both organisations found this exposure didn't help their brands.

I believe 'organisational culture' is the day-to-day lived experience of employees in the workplace, whether they feel they belong and want to continue working for that organisation. This means it is in the interests of organisations to get the culture right if they want to create an environment that encourages people to stay.

There is another factor worth noting. Society is changing rapidly. We now have four different generations in the workplace: Baby Boomers (born between 1946 and 1964), Generation X (born between

1965 and 1976), Millennials (born between 1977 and
1997) and Generation Z (born after 1997). Each of
these generations have very different expectations,
life experiences and different social influences. If we
take Millennials and Generation Z, they are tech-
savvy because technology is far more integrated
into their daily life. They also have different views
on authority. If organisations want to attract and
retain Millennials or Generation Z employees, they
have to make sure that the type of culture in their
organisation appeals to those generations.

Society is also becoming more diverse. An ageing
workforce means there will be increased disability in
the workplace as older employees become physically
challenged during their longer working lives. They
may start losing their vision or develop hearing or
mobility problems. The UK's ethnicity diversity is
also shifting. According to the McGregor-Smith
Review (2017)[2] 'In 2016, 14% of the working age
population [were] from a BME background. This
is increasing, with the proportion expected to rise
to 21% by 2051. However, this is not reflected in
most workplaces, with many ethnic minorities
concentrated in lower paying jobs.' It is important for

---

2   McGregor-Smith, Baroness (Feb 2017) 'Race in the Workplace: The
     McGregor-Smith Review', www.gov.uk/government/publications
     /race-in-the-workplace-the-mcgregor-smith-review

organisations to be mindful of their present culture so that they can adapt for the future in order to attract and retain people.

Organisations are increasingly global. They must reflect not only the customers they serve, but also their potential employee talent pools. These might consist of remote staff found through the gig economy, or people working for an outsourced organisation based in another continent.

Although an organisation may be UK-based, if it operates internationally it will have to be even more culturally aware and culturally intelligent. Your customers might not be just down the road. They might be on the other side of the world.

What is culture?

I find it difficult to get to grips with what culture is because it is so vast. It is not a tangible thing that you can put your finger on. I see culture as the sum of behaviours within the workplace, or as I described earlier, the day-to-day experience of employees. When I turn up at work, I expect to feel and see the culture. That's because we can see the culture around us through things like symbols, behaviours and structures. But it is also what is unseen. The unspoken norms and behaviours that surround us. That's why it's so difficult to define culture.

In 'The Leaders Guide to Corporate Culture' in the *Harvard Business Review*[3], the authors list the common characteristics of culture:

1. Culture is shared. It is something that everybody experiences in the organisation through its unwritten rules.

2. It is pervasive. It exists at every level of the organisation, through both its visible and invisible characteristics.

3. It is enduring. In the article, the authors identify Benjamin Schneider's 'attraction-selection-attrition' model, which describes how people are drawn to organisations with characteristics that are similar to their own. They state that 'organisations are more likely to select individuals who seem to fit in and, over time, those who do not fit in tend to leave. Thus, culture becomes the self-reinforcing social pattern that grows increasingly resistant to change and outside

---

3   Groysberg, B, Lee, J, Price, J, and Cheng, J. Yo-Jud (Jan–Feb 2018) 'The Leader's Guide to Corporate Culture: How to manage the eight critical elements of organizational life.' *Harvard Business Review* 96, no. 1, p44–52

influences.' I have witnessed hiring managers saying before even meeting a candidate that they don't think they are going to be a culture fit for the organisation or their team. This is an extremely subjective way of shortlisting candidates for an interview. Candidates should be selected on objective skills and their alignment with organisational and team values.

4. Finally, culture is implicit. It is something we recognise and respond to instinctively.

Culture is the sum of our small behaviours. It is usually the small things that have a bigger impact. These include norms, micro-inequities, unconscious bias and privilege, discussed in the previous chapter. These four behaviours contribute to a culture where people can feel they are not included. If an organisation has a particular culture which it projects to the outside world, it is going to attract the same kinds of people. It means that it is failing to attract diversity.

How culture affects diversity and inclusion

There are numerous models of organisational culture which you can apply to your organization. They all have their pros and cons and there is no crystal ball to let you see how they might impact on your organisation. I believe it is vital to select a model that gives you a framework to work with and a process to follow.

The one that I particularly like is the Edgar Schein model of organisational culture.[4] Schein was born in 1928 and is a former professor at the MIT Sloan School of Management, specialising in the field of organisational management. The reason I like Schein's model is because there is a close correlation between his cultural organisational model and what we need to think about in terms of diversity and inclusion. Schein talks about three important issues in his model: artefacts, values and assumed values. Let's look for a moment at how this model can be applied to the culture of an organisation, particularly through the lens of diversity and inclusion.

Artefacts

Artefacts are the visible aspects of a workplace, such as dress code. Your dress code might not be inclusive for gender-fluid people. If you have somebody in your organisation whose gender identity changes

---

4   Edgar Schein model, www.managementstudyguide.com/edgar -schein-model.htm

from day to day, one day identifying as male and the next as female, they might want to show up to work as either male or female on either of those days. Your dress code or uniform code may not accommodate this.

Open-plan offices are artefacts. They may not be inclusive for autistic people who have sensitivities to sound or light. They might find it difficult working in a busy, open-plan office with artificial light and background noise. Organisations that can provide different types of workspaces such as a mixture of quiet, reflective spaces and open-plan or team-collaboration spaces to work in will be more flexible.

Toilets are also artefacts. A lack of gender-neutral toilets, or disabled toilets, suggests a non-inclusive environment. As I described previously, one of the reasons I left an organisation was because they didn't have enough disabled toilets. Going to the toilet was a hassle. I often had to wait to get into the disabled toilet and it meant I was late for meetings. This experience didn't feel inclusive.

Values

In Chapter One we talked about the need to align diversity and inclusion to values. Organisations tend to have one or two values applicable to diversity and inclusion. Others might have values that are far more explicit, for example, 'We value diversity'. Which of your organisational values are supportive of diversity and inclusion? Remember that the values of an organisation contribute to the culture.

Assumed values

Assumed values are unspoken, but they still affect organisational culture. An example of this is presenteeism or expecting people to work late. If these are assumed values in an organisation, they can affect people with caring responsibilities or who have medical conditions. These include employees with elderly parents, parents who have to leave early to pick their children up, employees with a fluctuating health condition who need to go home early for therapy. I have also seen strange assumed behaviours in response to this culture. Staff who feel unable to leave work before their boss. Employees who leave their jackets on the back of their chairs to give the illusion that they are still at work but who have gone home for the evening.

Artefacts, values and assumed values create culture. Key to creating a more inclusive culture is finding a model that works best for the organisation. I like the Schein model because it is simple, and because of how it connects and overlaps with diversity and inclusion. To understand how your culture affects your organisation, pick a model and implement it from a diversity and inclusion point of view.

The importance of senior leadership

If an organisation is serious about examining its culture, it needs to make sure that everybody feels they belong and create an environment where people can thrive. I began the chapter by saying that all organisations thrive when their people thrive. When they put people before profit. But it needs to be done in an inclusive way. This is why senior leadership is so important in setting the workplace culture. Senior staff must be on board and demonstrate authentic, inclusive leadership. They set the tone of the whole organisation and have enormous influence over organisational culture. They have to 'walk the talk'.

If the senior staff get the culture right, they create a huge amount of energy that inspires people towards a common purpose or a shared goal. I believe that culture and leadership are intrinsically linked. Culture is something that a senior leader can't delegate to the HR department. It is up to every single leader in the business to create the culture. It is important to review an organisation's culture in line with diversity and inclusion so that it is future-proofed. What culture do you want in five- or ten-years' time? Society is constantly changing. As the workforce demographics and psychographics change, so too will the culture of the organisation.

You can view culture as a lever that is at the leaderships' disposal. Leaders can control a strategy and they can also influence culture. Academics and researchers have shown that culture is made up of the sum of everyone in the business. As it is so pervasive, culture can be managed and changed. When you think about the tangible things in your diversity and inclusion strategy, consider the kind of culture that you want to underpin your strategy.

Creating an inclusive culture in five easy steps

Creating an inclusive culture doesn't have to be complicated. It can be done in five easy steps:

1. Choose a model

2. Articulate the type of culture you want

3. Pick leaders that will lead the charge to change your culture

4. Increase organisational conversation

5. Reinforce through organisational structure and design

Step # 1: Choose a model

An organisation needs to choose a model or a framework to take them through logical steps as to how they design and implement their culture. Again, there are many models that all have their pros and cons. The model developed by Harvard-based Boris Groysberg, Jeremiah Lee, Jesse Price and Yo-Jud Cheng is another of my favourites.[5] Their model deals with eight different types of company culture. These types are plotted on an X and Y axis, X being how people interact and Y being their response to change. People interaction is measured on a scale of Independence to Interdependence. Response to change is measured against Stability to Flexibility.

The eight types of culture are:

---

5   Groysberg, B, Lee, J, Price, J, and Cheng, J. Yo-Jud (Jan–Feb 2018) 'The Leader's Guide to Corporate Culture: How to manage the eight critical elements of organizational life.' *Harvard Business Review* 96, no. 1, p44–52

- caring

- purpose

- learning

- enjoyment

- results

- authority

- safety

- order

What is interesting about this model is that the researchers discovered that the top-ranking cultures were 'results' and 'caring', which you would think are at opposite ends of the spectrum. The 'purpose' culture only accounted for 9% of the companies that they looked at. But if you consider millennials in the workplace, they are motivated by organisations with a higher purpose. Although it might not be my first choice, it reinforces one of my earlier points about how we need to be intentional about the culture we want to achieve. If that is the culture that younger employees are asking for, then we need to adapt and be flexible. Think about how to make everyone feel valued. Whether your employees are millennials, Generation X or Z, or Baby Boomers, they all bring value to the business. When we think about culture, we need to create a culture that encompasses everyone.

Step #2: Purposefully articulate the type of culture you want

Revisit your original diversity and inclusion strategy which we discussed in Chapter One. Use it to articulate the type of culture you want to create to support your diversity and inclusion strategy. Remember to select the appropriate language for your business. When I worked at a well-known consultancy firm, we talked about a culture of 'respect'. Many organisations talk about 'belonging'. One of my recent projects was analysing employee-inclusion survey results to see how we could make my client's organisation more inclusive. It was interesting to see that when people talked about the culture of the organisation, they used words such as 'supportive', 'friendly' and 'welcoming'. These are intrinsically linked to inclusion. If employees are already using these terms, why not formalise them? Adopt these words as your values. Use this language to describe your culture, especially if it supports diversity and inclusion.

Step #3: Pick leaders who will lead the charge to change your culture.

Not every leader in the business will be 100% behind diversity and inclusion. Some leaders will intuitively get it. They understand the various cases for supporting diversity and recognise why an inclusive workplace is essential for an organisation's future. These are the leaders that you want at the forefront. They are the early adopters: the champions of your diversity and inclusion strategy.

Step # 4: Increase organisational conversation

Once your leadership is on board, you need to build up the conversation across the whole of the business. Increase the amount of internal communications, talk about why culture is important, ask what kind of culture people want, make clear how you expect people to behave. Explain why diversity and inclusion is important to the organisation, and how the culture will support it. The leaders need to walk the talk; they need to go out on the 'shop floor' and talk to employees. They need to embody the desired behaviours required to create a more inclusive culture. Both their words and body language need to reflect this when they interact with people in the workplace and outside the organisation.

What about changing the visible aspects, or artefacts, of your organisation, as described in the Schein model? By installing gender neutral toilets or changing the office layout to accommodate the needs of both introverts and extroverts, or people on the autistic spectrum, you demonstrate how serious you are about becoming inclusive.

Make sure that the images used in marketing or recruitment material reflect that you are diverse. Leaders should also challenge the unseen norms (perhaps a female being expected to take the minutes in a meeting), not just those norms we take for granted (such as turning up to a meeting on time, or adhering to a deadline). Some micro-behaviours might be considered acceptable in the workplace, but leaders need to be bold and ask, 'Hang on a minute. Do we want this type of behaviour in our organisation?'

Step #5: Reinforce through organisational structure and design

To create a more inclusive workplace you need to hardwire inclusion into your organisational infrastructure as well as into your culture. Maybe, you should monitor the diversity of employees at each stage of your performance and development process to see where bias exists. We discuss this in greater detail in Chapter Four on Colleague Experience and Design which gives you methodologies for doing this.

How to become an inclusive leader

This chapter is about culture, but inclusive leadership is so intrinsically linked to inclusive culture that we need to be crystal clear on what we mean by 'inclusive leadership'. Juliet Bourke and Bernadette Dillon (Partner and Director respectively at Deloitte) have created 'The Six Signature Traits of Inclusive Leadership' which deliver that clarity.[6]

If you are serious about creating an inclusive culture you need to be very intentional about the culture you want to create to future-proof your organisation. As the leader, you are the custodian of that culture. You have personal responsibility for defining and shaping that culture and making sure that it is as

---

6   Bourke, J and Dillon, B (2016) 'The Six Signature Traits of Inclusive
     Leadership', www2.deloitte.com/us/en/insights/topics/talent/six
     -signature-traits-of-inclusive-leadership.html

inclusive as it can be. To be an inclusive leader you must give people confidence and inspire them to do their best work. It is not about command and control. It is about treating people fairly and with respect. It is about valuing the uniqueness in every single person and creating a sense of belonging. This is what good inclusive leaders do.

Bourke and Dillon identify the following six characteristics of inclusive leaders:

- They believe in diversity and inclusion

- They have courage

- They are aware of their biases and blind spots

- They are curious

- They have cultural intelligence

- They are collaborative

Let's delve into each in turn.

Inclusive leaders believe in diversity and inclusion

They understand the Business case for diversity and inclusion (discussed in Chapter One). They understand that an inclusive and diverse workplace will boost organisational performance and growth. They intuitively just get it. It's a gut feeling. Perhaps they have experienced it personally. They might be from a minority group themselves, or they could be thinking about their own sons or daughters. What if their daughter is really interested in technology, but isn't being encouraged down this route by the educational system? How would their autistic son cope in the workplace? Just as diversity and inclusion is intrinsically linked with the core values of an organisation, it is also embedded in the values of the senior leaders. Their own personal values of fairness, or openness or collaboration mean they are naturally inclusive leaders.

They have courage

Inclusive leaders are aware of their own strengths and weaknesses. They are also prepared to speak out and challenge behaviours in others that are not inclusive. They are happy to rock the boat in the organisation. When they see processes, systems or cultures that are not inclusive, they speak out. They challenge the status quo to make improvements to the business.

They are aware of their biases and blind spots

These leaders are aware of their own biases and blind spots that might affect their decision-making and the potential consequences for other people. They can also detect biases within processes and systems. For instance, they might see that the recruitment process is not particularly inclusive. Perhaps the organisation has a habit of recruiting graduates from the same small pool of universities. Work experience placements might always go to the relatives of senior staff (increasing nepotism). All of this affects diversity. The inclusive leader will question why they don't recruit from other universities where they can find a greater diversity of talent. If you want to be aware of your own biases, remember the **SEEDS** model from the previous chapter: **S**imilarity bias, **E**xperience bias, **E**xpedience bias, **D**istance bias and **S**afety bias.

Inclusive leaders know that you cannot treat everyone the same. I already mentioned the impact of privilege bestowing a head start. People start the race at different points. As a disabled person, if you treated me like everybody else in the team, I would actually be at a disadvantage. Because of the limitations I have with my disability, I need a leader who is flexible and able to adapt to me personally. During Ramadan you might have Muslim colleagues who are fasting. Their energy levels might not be the same as non-fasting colleagues. An inclusive leader understands and is responsive to this situation. They can flex and adapt how they manage their team so that the work can still be done without undue stress on a particular member. In one organisation, a young woman with a sleeping disorder was in the administration team. The repetitiveness of printing documents made her drowsy. She was advised that she could slip off at any time to a quiet room to rest and return to her tasks when she was able. Just knowing she could do this kept her a fully functioning and effective member of the team.

They are curious

Inclusive leaders are generally open-minded. They are more inquiring and ask open-ended questions. They are open to other people's points of view and are interested in world views. They never shut down an idea without exploring it further first. In my training sessions, I encourage people to say 'Yes, and...?' rather than blocking ideas and suggestions with words such as 'Why?' or 'No' or 'But'.

They have cultural intelligence

Inclusive leaders are adaptable; they flex their
style to different cultures. If they are working in an
international team, they can adapt to the various
cultures working within the organisation. They
recognise, understand and value cultural differences.
Their cultural intelligence score, which is also known
as 'CQ', is high. The BBC is a good example of an
organisation with several different cultures within
its individual divisions. The cultures in Design and
Engineering, Radio and News are very different; and
that's just within one organisation. A leader at the top
of an organisation like this needs to adapt their style
appropriately to interact effectively with all of the
differing cultures.

They are collaborative

Inclusive leaders encourage autonomy in people,
empowering them, and valuing their diversity of
thought. To foster collaboration, they create a sense
of psychological safety that encourages people in
teams to contribute as much as they can and to speak
up. This is essential. Being an inclusive leader is
about challenging the status quo of behaviours or
actions that are not inclusive. If they can instil this in

their team by creating that psychological safety, it is a very powerful tool for change.

The culture of an organisation is paramount. I could devote a whole book to it. The models I have presented for creating a positive culture are based on extensive research of available frameworks and on my own experience. I have worked with many organisations to help them create an inclusive culture that all employees can feel part of. These models are simple to use and effective. You just need the right ingredients, starting with inclusive leaders.

CASE STUDY: DELOITTE

'We had this group of people in the organisation who we could see we were losing, and they were telling us it was culture.'
— Emma Codd, Global Special Advisor on Inclusion at Deloitte

In her role as Managing Partner for Talent at Deloitte UK (2013–19), Emma played a leading role in the development of diversity, respect and inclusion. Based on this experience, Emma advocates a focus on what she describes as 'the million-dollar question'. This is how leaders can shape organisational culture to attract, recruit and retain a diverse workforce.

Gender Balance

In the previous decade a key inclusion aim for Deloitte was to improve gender balance in the workforce. To achieve this objective, Emma says the company had 'various programmatic initiatives', including setting up diversity networks in 2006–7.

Emma took on a leading role in 2013, but when reviewing the data in 2014, she saw that these initiatives, while positive, hadn't made a meaningful or sustained difference. 'Indeed, what you saw was some data going in the wrong direction.'

To understand what lay behind the trend, Emma analysed the exit data. This revealed the two main reasons people were leaving the company: work-life balance and culture. These themes became most evident when viewed from a gender perspective.

Emma set up listening groups. Made up of women and minority groups in the organisation, participants answered questions about their experience:

- How does it feel to work here?

- What is causing you to think about going elsewhere?

- What made your friends leave?

These activities confirmed that the major factors in people leaving the organisation were work-life balance and culture. They also enabled the firm to better understand what was meant by 'culture' when it was cited in the exit interviews.

Culture as Behaviour

Emma is clear. 'To me, culture is behaviour. What you are on the receiving end of and what you show to others. We had this group of people in the organisation who we could see we were losing, and they were telling us it was culture.' The listening groups identified that part of the culture problem was those everyday non-inclusive behaviours that can have a huge impact.

Emma gives an example. The Working Parents Transitions Coaching Programme supports parents returning to work. 'You sit there, you have this group and you get an amazing experience talking to others who feel like you do about coming back to work. Then people go back into work having set their personal parameters for successful work-life balance as a parent and someone in authority makes a comment about the employee leaving at 5pm to go home and get their kids.' That one behaviour undoes the previous good work of the programme.

Emma worries that inclusion is becoming a buzzword like diversity a few years earlier. Despite the focus, she questions the impact. 'Back in 2014, the minute I said diversity, people would say we've got the networks and we've done this and this.' At the same time the data told a different story. 'I was convinced we would never achieve this diversity of culture we wanted unless we had an inclusive culture, underpinned by respect. We looked at the everyday behaviours such as people passing comment on personal choices: the way someone looks or their beliefs. Well-meaning people thinking it was OK to do so. Not realising it was wrong.'

'There's a lot of talk about unconscious bias training, but what shows that it works? That's not the answer. Programmes on their own are not the answer or solution.'

Inclusive DNA

Deloitte defined its inclusive culture as one of respect. Emma says that 'Until organisations are in a position to have fully respectful and inclusive cultures, we will not crack diversity.' She also says that embedding respect and an inclusive culture is an interesting journey. Organisations often leave this job to the diversity and inclusion manager or the diversity networks, but to be successful Emma says 'inclusion has to be the DNA of your organisation, led from the top.'

REFLECTION

Take a few moments to answer the following questions:

1. How easily can you articulate why culture is important?

2. What cultural aspects in your organisation might not support an inclusive workplace?

3. Is your senior leadership team fully on board with creating a more inclusive culture? If not, how do you plan to engage them in this?

4. How might you define your organisational culture now? How could you create a plan of action to shift the culture to be more inclusive?

5. What are the steps that you can personally take to become a more inclusive leader?

In Chapter Three we learn how to implement changes to create a diverse and inclusive culture and the challenges that those responsible will face from above and below them in the organisation. Taking a change management approach is the first step to solving this issue.

THREE

Change

Taking a change management approach

Organisations need to treat diversity and inclusion in the same way as any other business change. When a new HR system like Workday or SAP is being introduced, or if there is a new strategy to relocate people, a proper change management project is immediately put in place with the appropriate controls and rigour. But when it comes to diversity and inclusion, I rarely see the same level of rigour applied. By not having proper change management in place, diversity and inclusion initiatives become piecemeal and are not joined up. This means organisations haven't defined what success looks like and don't know what impact is being made. Change is slow. People lose interest because more important and urgent issues keep coming down the line. The day-to-day job gets in the way, consuming time and energy. Diversity and inclusion is put on the back burner. Those who want to see change happen are disheartened because the process is so slow. They become disillusioned with an organisation that appears disinterested in becoming more inclusive and lacking direction.

Some organisations are lucky enough to employ a Diversity and Inclusion Manager. These managers often burn out quickly. They find themselves caught between the senior leader who is passionate to see change happen and is cracking the whip, the managers who are expected to implement the change, and those lower down the organisation who aren't feeling change happening fast enough. Diversity and inclusion changes take time. Even if you introduce diversity at the recruitment stage, and support new employees as they develop through the organisation, it will take years to diversify your pipeline of senior leaders.

There are several questions that organisations need to ask themselves when they are thinking about implementing diversity and inclusion:

1. Why do they want to become more diverse and inclusive?

2. What are they going to change?

3. How are they going to implement the change required?

4. Who is involved in that change?

5. When will the changes happen?

6. How do they know they have been successful?

The first two questions were answered in Chapters One and Two. In this chapter we deal with the other questions which are key to ensuring an organisation introduces diversity and inclusion in a structured and successful manner.

The key point is that organisations need to treat diversity and inclusion with much more rigour. They need to apply a change management approach as with any other organisational change. This means they need to:

- develop business cases and calculate return on investment or return on inclusion

- undertake a SWOT analysis to understand the strengths, weaknesses, opportunities and threats of the project

- Conduct a PESTLE analysis to understand the wider context in which diversity and inclusion operates. Consider the Political, Environmental, Social, Technological, Legal and Environmental forces impacting upon the diversity and inclusion of your organisation

- Use the RACI index to identify who is Responsible, Accountable, Consulted and Informed in effecting change (we analyse this later in the chapter)

- develop a robust communications strategy

- produce a clear delivery roadmap

- define how they measure the success of the project

- figure out how the initial change project becomes business as usual and part of the DNA of your organization

These actions are often missing from diversity and inclusion projects.

This is not an HR issue

Let's deal with the thorny issue of who is responsible for diversity and inclusion change. It is usually seen as HR's responsibility to drive and implement diversity and inclusion. It seems like the logical place for it to reside because diversity and inclusion is essentially about people and the workforce. But diversity and inclusion touches every single part of the organisation. This means that HR needs to work closely with every single department in the organisation. Very often diversity and inclusion is delegated to the HR department by the Chief Executive Officer (CEO) and two things happen. Either they don't take any interest, in which case, diversity and inclusion is swallowed up with everything else that's on the HR Director's desk. It doesn't get the time or attention it deserves and nothing happens. Or you have a hugely passionate CEO who doesn't delegate properly and ends up meddling and telling the HR department what to do. This overloads the HR Director or the Diversity and Inclusion Manager. You need a balance between a senior leader, ideally the CEO, who is passionate about driving the diversity and inclusion agenda (and is ultimately accountable for it) and whoever they make responsible for delivery.

I wouldn't deny that HR takes on most of the work for diversity and inclusion. They are responsible for the Reasonable Adjustments process for accommodating disabled employees or disabled candidates in the recruitment process to enable them to perform as well as they can in their roles. They are also responsible for the Employee Value Proposition, the Performance and Development process and on-boarding of new employees. These are all touch points for greater inclusivity. When it comes to performance and development, using the 9-box (3x3) grid described by James Brook in his article 'Unpacking myths underpinning the 9-Box Talent Grid', I rarely find people from minority backgrounds in the high performing, high potential 'star player' boxes[1]. This could be the consequence of unconscious bias or something systemic.

Diversity and inclusion is everyone's business no matter what department they work in. The Recruitment team is responsible for attracting people from the marketplace and encouraging them to apply. They guide applicants through the recruitment process in an inclusive way, so that everyone has an equal opportunity to get into the organisation. The Workplace team is responsible for managing buildings. As the buildings need to be as accessible as possible, they are also responsible for diversity and inclusion. Security teams are often situated front of house. They greet a diverse range

---

1   Brook, J (not dated) *Unpacking myths underpinning the 9-Box Talent Grid*', www.strengthscope.com/unpacking-myths-underpinning -9-box-talent-grid

of people coming through the door. They need to be as inclusive and welcoming as possible. The Procurement team is responsible for monitoring the supply chain for supplier diversity. How many suppliers are owned by women or have a female Chief Executive? How many are run by someone from an ethnic minority background? Or with a disability? The Technology department provides assistive technology to employees and also have a remit for diversity and inclusion. I can't use my arms and hands; I need to use speech-to-text software. It is the Technology department's responsibility to ensure that they have licences for the software and that it is on hand for any new employees so they can be productive as soon as possible. Technology allows flexible working. This helps working parents, people with fluctuating health conditions and those who are anxious commuting during rush hour. It is the Technology department's responsibility to provide everyone with a laptop and a smartphone to connect to the organisation's systems wherever they work from. The Internal Communications team needs to ensure that everybody can read their material in whichever format. This ranges from the choice of fonts, the accessibility of digital systems, to using simple, plain language that everybody can understand.

Diversity and inclusion applies to all areas of an organisation, whether Workplace, Security, Procurement, Technology, Internal Communications or HR. Diversity and inclusion is everyone's responsibility, not just HR's. However, given the range of departments involved, HR has to orchestrate the work through collaboration and engaging and influencing all the other departments to bring them on the journey.

HS2, the high-speed UK railway project, is particularly good at this. HS2 is a small organisation but it is delivering one of the largest railway engineering projects in the UK. They have been very careful about their supplier process and how organisations win projects on HS2. A large contributing factor for the weighting of project awards, includes actions taken by bidders regarding diversity and inclusion. If a company is not addressing diversity and inclusion, it could heavily influence their bid. Once a contract is awarded, it includes conditions regarding what the supplier proposes to do to improve diversity and inclusion. HS2 will carry out spot checks to ensure this is actually carried out.

The RACI Index

When I work with clients on their diversity and inclusion strategy, I encourage them to complete the RACI Index that is commonly used in stakeholder planning and management.[2] RACI stands for **R**esponsible, **A**ccountable, **C**onsulted and **I**nformed. Each applies to one quadrant of a grid. Let's look at each quadrant.

Responsible

In the Responsible quadrant, you list all those who are responsible for doing the work and hitting the milestones for the changes. These people are responsible for making the change happen. They should be the senior leaders from each of the departments we mentioned, who can influence and drive the change. They may have support. Perhaps an HR director will engage an HR business partner to organise meetings and execute projects.

---

2   RACI Index, https://en.wikipedia.org/wiki/Responsibility
     _assignment_matrix

Accountable

The people listed in the Accountable quadrant are those whose neck is on the line if change doesn't happen. Ideally it includes the CEO who will drive the change from top down. Or it could be a senior leader who reports to the CEO, such as the HR Director or Chief Operating Officer. It is important that this person has influence across all departments and does not just focus on the HR department.

Consulted

List the people in this quadrant who you will consult to get feedback about their experiences of working in the organisation. You also want to get their opinions on what the organisation should do to improve diversity and inclusion. They tend to be named individuals and people you regularly consult such as the person who runs your LGBT+ employee network. Or you might want to consult with an outside expert like me. You should also list the groups of people you need to consult – employees, and employee resource groups such as LGBT+ networks, disability networks, gender networks or ethnicity networks. You might also want to consult suppliers and customers who often get forgotten. It is essential that customers are included in any diversity and inclusion strategy to ensure that it reflects the diversity of your customer base. Strategic partners will also be listed. Many organisations outsource IT Support or their Finance Service Desk or their HR Help Desk. These service providers need to understand how important diversity and inclusion are to your organisation and know how they can assist in achieving those goals. You might also include alumni in this quadrant as they can provide valuable feedback.

Informed

Middle managers are often overlooked and should be listed in the Informed quadrant. This group frequently gets caught between the passion of senior leaders who understand diversity and inclusion (and the direction the organisation needs to take) and junior employees who want change to happen quickly. Middle managers are responsible for implementing the changes and it is vital to keep this group engaged in the process.

Kotter's Change Management Model

Even though organisations want to implement diversity and inclusion change, I often find that they lack a structure or a formula to help drive that change forward. They need a change model that is simple and allows them to answer the following questions:

- Where are we now?

- Where do we want to be?

- What are we thinking or doing that's holding us back?

- What obstacles might get in our way?

- What do we need to do in order to get there?

My favourite change model is Kotter's Theory.[3] There are eight stages in this model which we will examine in turn.

1. Create a sense of urgency

This is essential because diversity and inclusion is generally not regarded as high priority. It gets pushed aside by more urgent matters. Every day I talk to HR directors who are constantly firefighting: dealing with grievances, redundancies, relocations, reward, performance management, workforce

---

3   Kotter, J, 'Eight Step Process for Leading Change', www.kotterinc .com/8-steps-process-for-leading-change

planning and succession. No wonder diversity and inclusion remains at the back of the queue. The CEO should be responsible for creating a sense of urgency. They need to create a simple narrative that touches the nerve of the organisation as to why diversity and inclusion is important. Create two or three talking points and complete a SWOT and PESTLE analysis. This will give you a full understanding of the issues you are dealing with. Gather a high energy, core group of people who can get things done quickly – a handful of passionate, influential but pragmatic people. What you don't want is a group of passionate people with little influence in the organisation and who lack structure. While they might sponsor the local Pride festival, they won't tackle the day-to-day problems that LGBT+ employees face in the organisation. Your core team can build a head of steam and make a quick impact.

2. Build a core coalition

As mentioned previously, senior people from all departments, not just HR, need to take responsibility for diversity and inclusion. This step ensures that these departments work collaboratively. It includes HR, IT, Procurement, Security, Recruitment, Marketing, Internal Communications, etc. Senior management are the influencers who can persuade stakeholders and others to get on board.

3. Form a strategic vision

The next step is to create your strategic vision. This will be done by the core team. The strategy needs to be simple and address the following questions:

- Where are we now?

- Where do we want to get to?

- What are we thinking or doing that's holding us back?

- What obstacles might get in our way?

- How are we going to get there?

Chapter One covered strategy development and the importance of using language that everyone understands. You need to discuss the results you expect to see and the benefits you hope to achieve before moving on to the next step.

4. Get everybody on board

It's time to get the rest of the organisation excited and on board with the change. This includes a constant stream of internal communications. Sending one email or convening one town hall won't work. Regular communication is required, ideally from the CEO. Not everyone will get what you are trying to achieve immediately. It is essential that the messages are delivered in a variety of accessible formats to engage all staff and increase their understanding. This includes emails, newsletters, social media and posters in the workplace. Think about investing in merchandise for the office: cups, coasters, mouse mats. I worked in one organisation that did this so effectively that an employee said that they felt confident coming out to work colleagues after seeing one of the Senior Leadership team walking around the office with an LGBT+ ally mug in their hand.

5. Reduce barriers and remove friction

Revisit your RACI Index and check who is in the Responsible quadrant. Ensure you have the right people with the right knowledge and skills to effect change. This may mean they need training on diversity and inclusion. Make sure the right level of budget is allocated to the project. Many organisations don't fund diversity and inclusion projects adequately and expect the strategy to be delivered on a shoestring. Nothing is for free, and

I appreciate that some organisations have bigger pockets than others. But if an organisation is prepared to put their money where their mouth is, it sends out the signal that they are serious about diversity and inclusion. You also encounter the problem of people having to carry out this work in addition to their day jobs. Which means they can become overstretched and change doesn't happen. Make sure you give people adequate time aside from their day job to deliver your strategy.

6. Create short-term wins

This gives the project momentum and instils confidence that change is on the way. Identify the short-term wins that you can achieve. Set your milestones and get change happening quickly.

7. Sustain acceleration

Once you've built momentum, not only do you need to keep it going, you need to reduce the risk of it losing steam. Diversity and inclusion changes can take a very long time; people can become demotivated, bored and lose faith that things are going to happen. People also change in an organisation. They move departments or leave. It is important to factor this in and identify ways to sustain change and keep it moving forward.

8. Set the stages in stone

Make sure diversity and inclusion changes become embedded in the organisational culture and infrastructure. This is discussed in the next chapter.

Kotter's theory for leading change is a good top-down model. The CEO needs to spearhead diversity and inclusion change. The model also focuses on the foot soldiers, the ones who deliver change. In my experience, they are people at the grassroots.

As with any model, there are disadvantages. A top-down model also needs a bottom-up approach. If an organisation uses Kotter's theory, they also need to consider how to build structure and rigour from the bottom up. They need to set parameters for what they expect from their employees. I know many employees who are passionate about inclusion and diversity. But 'doing their own thing' means they don't make a big overall impact. Activities need to be aligned with the organisation's strategy. Employees need to be informed of the boundaries to work within to keep in line with the structure.

Successful change management

If an organisation wants to be effective in implementing diversity and inclusion changes, there are several factors to consider. Firstly, an appropriate delivery mechanism needs to be in place. Without it you run the risk of senior leaders overloading the person responsible for implementing the change. Leaders who are passionate about change may continuously throw curve balls and wonder why things aren't happening. They might not realise that with every new idea they come up with, the person in charge has to switch tactics, move onto something else, leave things half-done. Nothing ever gets finished. The project leader burns out. The delivery plan doesn't need to be complicated. You can start by simply answering the following questions:

- What is the diversity and inclusion project we are going to implement?

- What is the desired goal of that project?

- What needs to be delivered as a result of that project?

- Who is accountable and responsible for delivering that project?

- When is it going to be delivered?

This doesn't require complicated software. A simple spreadsheet will do. This way you can keep your plan updated monthly.

Secondly, identify clear roles and responsibilities. Senior leaders must demonstrate that they trust the core team. Give them time and space to do the work. No meddling or micro-managing. Let them get on with it.

Thirdly, ensure an adequate budget is in place. Some organisations throw money at this. Other organisations don't have big budgets to play with. It is essential that a budget is allocated; if only to signal that the organisation is serious about diversity and inclusion. Putting money behind something means you are really investing in it. It's viewed as a priority across the organisation. Of course, a budget requires proper financial controls. Draw up a business case so that the return on investment and your return on inclusion are clear.

Deliver in an Agile way

After university I worked in technology, implementing IT systems, designing websites and apps. I learnt about project management of IT and software. One of the most effective methods I used for managing IT projects was Agile project management. I now use Agile in my work as a Diversity and Inclusion specialist.

It's not within the remit of this book to teach you about Agile. In fact, it would take a book in itself! But I want to demonstrate briefly the effectiveness of Agile. The traditional way of managing projects is over a long period, sometimes years. By the time you've delivered the project, your original requirements may have changed, and the project that you're delivering no longer meets the needs of the organisation.

Agile is a more responsive approach that easily adapts to an organisation's needs. Using Agile, you can deliver change faster and sooner. There are shorter feedback loops. The design, implementation, testing and delivery of a project are completed in a shorter timeframe. It is done in cycles so that by the time you get to the end of a cycle, you've delivered some sort of change and value and you know if you're on the right track. Before you proceed onto the next cycle you have the opportunity to adjust your plans.

Agile methodology was created around a set of principles that are just as effective for implementing diversity and inclusion change as for technology development. One principle is that the best solutions come from self-organising teams. Allow a project team that's responsible for implementing diversity and inclusion to self-organise and they will define the solutions that can be delivered to solve the relevant problems. Another principle that I like is prioritising conversation over documents. I worked for one organisation where I spent so much time writing business cases and getting agreement to them that it was impossible to get on with the work. Sometimes it felt like paralysis from analysis.

There are many resources on the internet to learn more about Agile.[4] I recommend that you take some time to review what is available and think how you can apply Agile principles to deliver diversity and inclusion changes effectively within your organisation.

---

4   For example, Agile Project Management, https://www.apm.org.uk /resources/find-a-resource/agile-project-management

CASE STUDY: NETWORK RAIL

'The discipline of project management ensures the successful implementation of organisational diversity and inclusion.'
— Loraine Martins, Director of Diversity and Inclusion at Network Rail

Prior to Network Rail, Loraine worked for the Olympic Delivery Authority (ODA) as the Head of Equality, Inclusion, Employment and Skills. Tasked with creating a more diverse workforce and delivering an accessible environment, including preparing for the legacy post the London 2012 Olympic Games, it proved a role in which Loraine evolved and refined her methodology.

Loraine now leads the strategic direction of Network Rail's approach to diversity and inclusion, a broad remit which encompasses:

- attracting, recruiting and retaining employees

- accessibility of the environment for staff and customers

- working with procurement function and organisations in the supply chain

- engaging with employees of the future

Championing change management

An advocate of a programme- and change-management approach to diversity and inclusion, Loraine became a 'convert' during her time with the ODA. She is clear that the discipline of project management ensures the successful implementation of organisational diversity and inclusion.

Loraine says that working on building the Olympic Park was a turning point. In construction, project management is key, with every stage planned to align with the next phase. Project planning interventions, alongside setting targets and milestones, introduces accountability when developing diversity and inclusion. Loraine feels that without this robust approach, diversity and inclusion can be seen as 'smoke and mirrors'.

Start with the why?

Before embarking on change, Loraine advises asking the big question, 'Why is this change important to the business?' She says the 'why' doesn't have to be complicated, but it should be a crisp narrative, underpinning the rationale from which everything else flows.

Relentless focus on the 'why' moves organisations away from thinking that diversity and inclusion is a nice thing to do and challenges the business to understand the benefits. The 'why' also helps to drive the communication strategy around change management, developing authentic engagement across the business.

Where are we now?

To plan for change, it's critical to understand the composition of the current workforce. It's important to understand who is in the environment, how they experience it and if an organisation is reflective of its community.

With a baseline, set ambitions, develop a strategy and produce specific, measurable targets. The timeline for delivery needs to be clear. Network Rail operates a diversity-and-inclusion strategy through a five-year programme.

Programming change

Those leading change-management programmes should ensure the following are in place from the outset of the project planning process: an understanding of organisational interdependencies, risk management capabilities and available resources.

Using a project management process enables diversity-and-inclusion practitioners to structure conversations with other parts of the business and leverage opportunities for collaboration. Loraine cites alignment with safety culture as an example at Network Rail. Tangible outputs contributing to business drivers develop alliances which amplify the diversity-and-inclusion voice across the organisation, something Loraine feels is imperative.

Whilst it may appear counterintuitive to a rigorous project-management approach to delivery, Loraine is an advocate of being able to be flexible in the programme, because it is all about people. The ability to shift interventions allows organisational learning about what works to take place and informs a contextualised response when activities may need adapting, pausing or bringing forward.

Tips for Diversity and Inclusion Practitioners

To achieve cultural change, involve everyone, from the CEO to operational staff. People engage with the change agenda at various levels of the organisation, but all have a role. Loraine describes diversity and inclusion as being the conductor of an orchestra. Employees may play different instruments, but everyone is reading the same score.

Loraine insists that knowing about project management and its tools is crucial. A solid plan will underpin the resilience needed to deliver the programme. Failing to plan is planning to fail. Loraine says practitioners should always know their plan inside out.

REFLECTION

1. What change-management model will help you create structure and steps to implement change?

2. How could you articulate to your colleagues why you need this structure and rigour to bring about diversity-and-inclusion changes?

3. Who is ultimately accountable for creating a more inclusive workplace (hint: your CEO)? Who is going to be responsible? Who will be consulted and who needs to be kept informed?

4. What needs to be in place to successfully deliver change?

5. How might a more Agile approach to implementing diversity-and-inclusion changes help your organisation? Could you get results sooner if you follow this approach?

In the next chapter we discuss how you can use human-centred design to build a more inclusive workplace now that you have some strong foundations for change management within your organisation.

FOUR

Colleague Experience And Design

Interventions that matter

In the previous chapters we talked about the need for culture change, along with the need to make targeted interventions where change is most needed. Organisations need to be careful that these targeted interventions are not simply short-term or box ticking measures that look good and win awards. They must create sustainable culture change in the organisation. Current interventions tend to be designed for specific groups. Organisations might run a leadership development programme for women and another one for people of an ethnic minority background. Or they might offer a course on agile and flexible working for parents, without opening it up to anyone else in the organisation.

They might sponsor the local Pride march or organise something for Black History month and think they've ticked the box.

But this can be ineffective and end up excluding people. I have recently become aware of rumblings in the marketplace. A concern that we are not engaging white straight men in the conversation; they are feeling left out, disenfranchised, disengaged and quite threatened by diversity. If there is one lesson I want you to take away from this book, it is that we need to take a more intersectional approach, something most organisations fail to do. We need to remember that diversity includes everyone.

Bear in mind that interventions designed by organisations are usually about fixing people and not necessarily about fixing the organisation, its culture, or its systems. A Women in Leadership Programme doesn't take account of systemic issues that might hold women back in their careers, such as a lack of flexible working or expectations that they have to work long hours, making it difficult to balance family life and work life. These programmes generally don't involve men's contribution to potential solutions by encouraging them to take a more active role in caring responsibilities which we know are a major factor in the gender pay gap.

Short-term interventions tend not to be strategically aligned, which is what we talked about in Chapter One, but they need to be. I believe that organisations who approach diversity and inclusion with short-term interventions are not making any progress. Many believe that diversity is going backwards, not improving. Certainly, the organisations I speak to say that diversity is stagnating or in some cases regressing. We have to stop and ask ourselves what the data is telling us. Are the actions we've taken actually making an impact? Do we need a completely different approach to implementing more diverse or inclusive workplaces?

I recently carried out some research among my network of HR directors and Diversity and Inclusion leaders. One of their biggest frustrations was that the pace of change was too slow. They were also frustrated that people expect change to happen quickly and expressed the need for patience on all sides. You cannot transform the diversity and inclusion of a company overnight. It takes time to create more inclusive workplaces. In practical terms, growing a pipeline of talent will take years not months, for people to develop and take on senior roles.

There is also the risk of this being used as an excuse. The organisations that impress me go into the public domain and make bold statements about their intentions. They are not scared of shaking things up. We talked about inclusive leaders who are not afraid to rock the boat. If organisations want to see progress, as many of them do, they need to be prepared to challenge the status quo. My argument is that we need a very different way of delivering diversity and inclusion. An organisational culture will only improve when we actually implement change. Otherwise we carry on doing the same things and we will still be talking about this in another ten years' time. When I talk to people who have been working in the industry for longer than me, they are disappointed that they are repeating the same things they were saying a decade ago. They see very little progress. Nothing is really shifting. Society is rapidly changing in terms of diversity and there's a huge opportunity cost for organisations that fail to tap into it.

We now have four generations of people working in the same workplace. Organisations have to be inclusive of all four. Not because it's the right thing to do, but because these four generations represent an experienced, highly skilled workforce. We need to leverage all their experiences and skills, whether they are a baby boomer or a generation Z just entering the workplace, full of creative ideas and experience of having grown up in a connected tech world. We need to bring everyone together. This requires a different way of being inclusive. That's why successful implementation of diversity and inclusion changes should be based on a human-centred approach.

It's time to take a human-centred approach

One of my favourite quotes is from Sergey Gladkiy:

> 'One of the key things around user-centred design is that it starts with human beings and ends with the answers that are tailored to their individual needs. When you understand the people you're trying to reach and then design from their perspective, you come up with unusual answers.'[1]

I particularly like it because it's about the human being. Diversity and Inclusion managers and HR Directors tend to think about cohorts of people. What do they need to do for the disabled? What do they need to do for people of an ethnic minority background? What do they need to do for aspiring

---

1   Gladkiy, S (June 2018) 'User-Centred Design: Process and Benefits', https://uxplanet.org/user-centered-design-process-and-benefits -fd9e431eb5a9

female leaders? Everyone is put into groups and they lose sight of individual needs, goals and aspirations. There is the risk of making assumptions and stereotyping people. They think 'This is what the disabled people need.' It has the effect of putting a group of people at arms' length rather than being inclusive.

I want to encourage taking a human-centred approach. Start from the perspective of the individual so you avoid the risk of thinking in silos. To do this within a diversity and inclusion context, you need to think about the journeys that an individual goes on in an organisation. What are the speed humps and roadblocks they might encounter? What is slowing them down or preventing them from completing a particular journey?

I know that HR directors might think that taking a human-centred approach and designing programmes for the specific needs of individuals might risk not meeting the needs of everyone else. I believe this is a false assumption. What you find is that if you design for a specific person in mind, someone you can name and describe in detail, by default you end up improving the working life or journey for everybody. As human beings we all share the same needs and desires. By taking this approach, by thinking about specific individuals and aiming to improve their journeys, you may find you can address the vast majority of other people's needs too.

The design agency IDEO are a leading authority on human-centred design. They say: 'Human-centred design is all about building a deep empathy with the people you're designing for, generating tonnes of ideas, building a bunch of prototypes, sharing what you've made with people you're designing for, and eventually putting your innovative new solution out to the world.' This draws on the previous chapter about change and the need to work in an Agile way. The value is in the implementation. You can implement quicker by getting feedback and adjusting your course of action as you progress. It's the same as implementing any new design solution. By using prototypes, testing and getting feedback, you implement what works. Contrast this with spending weeks, months, even years, analysing, designing and building, only to realise that by the time you implement the solution, the goalposts have moved and the solution is no longer fit for purpose.

Employee journeys

Employees go through many different journeys during their lifecycle in an organisation. These cover several key areas: entering the organisation, developing and remaining in the organisation, perhaps taking breaks for parental leave, sideways moves, promotions, other changes, and finally leaving the organisation. But there are two other journeys which are equally important. The one your suppliers take and your customers' journey. Within each journey there are several issues that an organisation must be aware of.

Let's look at each individual journey:

1. Entering the organisation

There are various touch points along this journey where diversity and inclusion needs to be guaranteed to make an individual feel welcomed. These are at recruitment, onboarding, and arranging any workplace adjustments.

Recruitment

When an organisation thinks about diversity and inclusion it usually focuses on the recruitment process. This is the obvious opportunity to get more diverse people through the door. It is essential to think through each step, from the moment someone is drawn to your organisation and inspired to apply to work for you, through the various interview stages or assessment stages to the final offer being made. By doing this, you ensure that each step is as inclusive as possible and everyone has an equal chance of success.

Onboarding

Once somebody accepts a job they usually go through the onboarding and induction stage. Organisations need to ensure this process is inclusive and everybody is welcomed and supported. People should feel that they belong to the organisation from day one.

Workplace adjustments

We have a duty under the Equality Act to make reasonable adjustments for disabled people, but I believe this should apply for everybody. If I am a working parent and I have to drop the kids off at school in the morning, then it would really help me if I had flexibility in terms of when I start my day. Perhaps I get anxious travelling on peak-time commuter trains. Starting work earlier would allow me to catch a quieter train. These are inclusive adjustments that would benefit everyone, not just one specific group of people.

2. Developing and remaining within the organisation

This second category of journey is about developing people, ideally promoting them and retaining them so that the organisation improves its retention scores. There are several ways to achieve this inclusively:

Project and work allocation

Do you know managers who always choose the same people to take on projects because they know they can rely on them? Why not allocate the work to someone who is untried and untested? It could be a career-defining project for them. If a rotational system of allocating work is adopted, everyone has an equal chance to excel, not just the chosen few.

Getting promoted

Similarly, there needs to be a fair, inclusive, transparent way of promoting people in the organisation. One of the biggest complaints I see from my clients' employee engagement results and surveys, is that there isn't a fair and transparent system or process for promotions and pay.

Reward and recognition

Another way to encourage people to stay is through reward and recognition for their work. To ensure inclusion, monitor the data to see if there is any disparity in terms of diversity. Data insights will grow your understanding of any gaps or disparities that need to be addressed. If you are reporting on the gender pay gap why don't you also calculate your ethnicity and disability pay gaps as well?

Performance and development

A system for performance and development is essential in any organisation to encourage retention of staff, but how inclusive is yours? How inclusive is the access to training and development? Do you have insights into the diversity of people who access training and development? What about your performance management process? If you have a quarterly or annual promotion cycle, how open or transparent are you about that? And do you have the data that shows if there are any inequalities on who is getting promoted?

Wellbeing and employee support

How inclusive is wellbeing and employee support in your organisation? One of my pet peeves is that lots of organisations provide employees with a pedometer to improve their physical wellbeing and encourage them to take 10,000 steps a day. A sign beside the lift says 'Please consider taking the stairs rather than the lift. You'll burn off X number of calories and save the planet because you're not using it.' As somebody in a wheelchair this doesn't strike me as particularly inclusive. A pedometer is completely inappropriate for me. It is important to ensure that your wellbeing activities are inclusive of different abilities, providing suitable support for all employees' health and wellbeing needs including those who aren't able or don't want to use pedometers, for instance.

3. Transitions and changes

Employees may work for an organisation for many years. It is inevitable that life happens to them and things change. Organisations need to support their employees when significant events occur in their lives.

Becoming a parent

Maybe they have become a first-time parent. They might want to reconsider working arrangements or adopt a flexible working pattern. They might want extended parental leave. Language is important in this situation to ensure inclusivity. Take care not to refer only to females (maternity, mothers, mums, etc). Parental leave includes fathers, same sex couples, those adopting a child or with caring responsibilities. Although women may still take on the majority of caring responsibilities, organisations can play a big part by talking more openly and sharing stories about the role that fathers or men play in caring for children. Families are all different and include single-parent families, same-sex couple families, etc. Parental policies should be inclusive, referring to parents rather than mums and dads. Language plays an important part in ensuring policies are fair and equal.

Relocating to another team or area

If an organisation is moving its operations to another location, is inclusivity being considered in the move? If your organisation plans to downsize or relocate, an equality impact assessment needs to be completed to see if any groups are adversely affected. For example, if you plan to relocate a whole office to another part of the UK or overseas, you need to consider how difficult it might be for disabled people to move because of their local support network such as their access to appropriate social care and healthcare. The organisation should ensure it understands the impact of the move on different people and put in place an inclusive action plan for relocating them

Acquiring a disability or a long-term health condition

According to the Shaw Trust on the Disabled Living Foundation website, 'Only 17% of disabled people were born with their disabilities. The majority of disabled people acquire their disability later in life.'[2] How supportive is the organisation at being able to adapt and provide adjustments to those individuals and support them physically and psychologically as they adjust to a new way of living and working?

Transitioning whilst at work

People frequently transition during their time in an organisation. By that I mean, a personal transition. This might be becoming a parent for the first time,

---

2   Shaw Trust (part of the Disabled Living Foundation), 'Key Facts', www.dlf.org.uk/content/key-facts

but it can be more far-reaching for someone who transitions as a transgender person. It can be a minefield for them. How do they broach the subject with their manager or their team? How do they show up for work for the first time with the identity that they would rather be seen by? If they need to take time out for treatments, how do they manage it? How do they balance this time out with their work? This is a subject that is rarely discussed in organisations. We need to think carefully about how we support these employees when they are going through a personal transition of this sort.

4. Leaving the organisation

Where people feel they've had a good experience working for an organisation, they will act as a champion for them. Good organisations recognise that ex-employees can become future clients and advocates. To ensure you are being inclusive, set up an exit process that includes ways capturing the views of those who leave. Good organisations will conduct exit interviews and take action on the feedback. Or they ask every leaver to complete a survey which is analysed and the data acted upon.

Becoming alumni

Some organisations develop an alumni network. Provided this is inclusive, it can make people feel they belong to a community and will participate and engage fully. If your organisation holds regular meet-ups, consider whether they are in wheelchair-accessible venues.

5. Supplying your organisation

An area often neglected is that of supplier diversity or supply-chain diversity.

Becoming a supplier

Thinking about your organisation now, what is your process for taking on new suppliers and how inclusive is it? Do you actively reach out to organisations that are run by minority groups?

Delivering services in an inclusive way

Do you work closely with your delivery partners to make sure that the services they deliver on your behalf are done in an inclusive way? For example, if you outsource your IT help desk to a technology company is their issue logging system accessible, are the technologists trained in different assistive technologies and have they had disability-confident training?

6. Customer journeys

It is crucial to understand the touch points your customers have with your organisation. Make sure each one is inclusive. If I want to get a mortgage I go onto the bank's website. If I can't access the website because it doesn't work well with screen readers (used by blind customers), how will I know what mortgages are available? If I have a learning disability, I might not understand the terms and conditions because they're not written in an inclusive way using plain English. If I want to visit my local branch to talk to somebody face-to-face, as a wheelchair user, what if there is a step into the building? That's why it is important to examine each touch point the customer has with your organisation to address any obstacles.

These are just a handful of potential journeys. If I spent time with you brainstorming your own user journeys and mapping them out on a whiteboard, you will be surprised how many journeys we could make more inclusive. It can feel quite overwhelming to fix every journey, so it's important to prioritise those that have the biggest impact.

Steps to taking a human-centred approach

There are five practical ways that organisations can take a human-centred approach to implementing diversity and inclusion:

1. Identify non-inclusive journeys

My experience tells me that you will find most journeys in your organisation are non-inclusive. Data and insights will help you prioritise the journeys to tackle first. If an organisation is going through rapid growth, it makes sense to focus on the recruitment processes. This is the best opportunity to get diversity through the door. Find a way of getting everybody engaged in the change you are proposing. Identify your change model and get your early adopters on board to fire up people's interest and involve them in implementing these changes.

2. The user context and needs

This step is about gathering information and feedback. Talk to people, conduct surveys and interviews, send out questionnaires and create focus groups. You want to fully understand the users' needs. I like undertaking ethnographic research. This means finding out how people feel about their workplace environment and day-to-day work life. It is a great way of understanding and documenting how people experience the organisation. Put yourself in the shoes (or wheels) of an employee, customer or supplier, and try to understand how they might feel about their different journeys.

If you are focusing on the recruitment process, try the 'mystery shopper approach'. Submit applications to jobs in other companies to find out what it's like going through their recruitment process. Or go to the Apple store and observe what it is like to be one of their customers. How is their customer service? How inclusive are they? I love going to five-star hotels. I find them inclusive and customer centric. To experience customer centricity at its best, go to a five-star hotel for afternoon tea and absorb the experience. Networking is another valuable source of information. Find out what's happening on Meetup. com. It has all kinds of networking groups. LGBT+

Professionals in the City, for instance, or different ethnic minority groups, or disability groups. You can talk to people about their own experiences in the workplace and find out what their working life is like.

Once you have gathered your information and insights, you can create 'scenarios'. These are fictional day-in-the-life stories of users. Think about a specific user journey and describe their best-case scenario rather than dwell on the negatives. Include emotions to bring the story to life.

3. The organisational requirements

Armed with this insight and information, you now need to make sure that you not only address the needs of the user but also of the organisation. Go back to the diversity and inclusion objectives that were discussed in Chapter One. Reflect on the targets that you set to ensure that what you are doing helps achieve that strategy and allows you to create the culture that you want. Think about how these user journeys support your organisational requirements and goals. Go for the positives. Don't say you need to reduce attrition but that you want to increase employee engagement or retention. This is a much more positive statement for employees.

4. Build solutions

Once you've covered the first three steps, it's time to design and build your solutions, ideally adopting an Agile approach. Get a diverse group of people to work on the project. A senior person will remove obstacles and act as a champion. A project manager will keep the project on track so that it maintains momentum. A mixed range of end users will contribute to how the project should be designed and delivered. Include employees who show potential. It can be an opportunity for them to shine and boost their careers.

This step is about co-design. It is not about the HR department coming up with its own plans, and then presenting them as the solution to employees. It needs a company-wide approach where you roll up your sleeves, get your hands dirty, work with colleagues to co-design and create together. It is an iterative approach where you test and deliver each step before moving on to the next. It involves engaging with employees. There might be a core team working on this (ideally multi-disciplinary). At regular intervals they consult their Diversity Networks and engage with employees to ask for their input to confirm they are on the right track. The core team should include a creative person and a logical technical person. You also need people from different departments such as HR, IT and Customer Service. They bring different perspectives and experiences. This means that the best solution possible is designed for your organisation.

5. Implement, test, review

Once you have your solutions, you need to implement them. There's nothing new about this stage, but it is vital to successful project management. Use a project-management approach to put your changes in place. Then constantly test your solution. Make sure you don't implement the wrong thing. Keep testing to make sure that it remains relevant. The world of work is rapidly changing. Implementing something doesn't mean that's it, you can tick a box and say you've fixed it. You have to keep reviewing and adjusting to keep up with changes in the world of work and society at large.

Diversity and inclusion is a living breathing thing. This book is about hardwiring it into an organisation. It's why you need to constantly review, adapt and adjust. You need to get to a point where these interventions are no longer seen as interventions, but just part of the way that things are done. When it's in the DNA of the organisation.

CASE STUDY: INTUIT

'You only find out what you need to know by asking people about the problem.'
— Ben Brown, Head of Engineering, Europe at Intuit QuickBooks

Intuit is a 35-year-old software company. It builds a range of products across small business and consumer spaces. Ben works on QuickBooks Online, an accounting product which has over 4.5 million global customers.

Scott Cook, Intuit's founder, embedded the company's customer-centric principles from the very beginning. A personal experience set the scene for this focus on customer experience. Quicken was Intuit's original personal accounting software product. Its inception was the solution to a domestic observation. Scott noticed that his wife was spending a lot of time and effort sitting at the kitchen table to manually balance her cheque book. This kitchen table is now installed at the Intuit Head Office in Mountain View, California. The table is a reminder that the company will always place the customer at the heart of everything they do.

The founding value to deliver beyond customer expectations drives everything Intuit does. This value is operationalised through their Design for Delight framework, otherwise known as D4D. Design for Delight is the articulation of three key principles which aim to deliver 'dramatic improvements in our customers' lives':

- **Principle 1: Deep Customer Empathy**

Ben describes this as taking the time to understand what the customer is experiencing, what the customer's problem is. This gives the company both the information and empathy to inspire innovation.

- **Principle 2: Go Broad to Go Narrow**

This is the process that Ben describes as 'What are all the possible solutions to this problem?' Having generated ideas, the process is to narrow these down to the best solution.

- **Principle 3: Rapid Experiments with Customers**

Rapid experimentation with customers is active testing of solutions to meet customer needs. The findings from this phase intentionally circle back to principle 1, providing real-life feedback before the end solution is built.

Scott Cook says that 'D4D is our number one secret weapon at Intuit. There is no number 2.'

Ben is clear that 'the culture at Intuit dictates that D4D should be in everything that we do and D4D is also used internally at Intuit. Intuit strongly aligns with the employee experience. It's important that the employee comes first. Amazing employee experience leads to amazing customer experience. This leads to successful shareholder returns.'

An example of using D4D internally is a recent office move. To align with D4D principles, the first step was to understand the needs of employees for their office space. Diversity and inclusion considerations arising from D4D was the need for gender-neutral toilets. 'Understanding that it matters to employees is critical.'

Ben says that when using D4D, the company always find something surprising in the process, giving the following example:

'One of the behaviours we are trying to change this year is to become more customer-obsessed. We were looking at trying to understand how customer-obsessed employees are. We interviewed employees and got them to self-rate out of 10 how customer-obsessed we are. The average range was between 7–10, so rating quite high.'

We also asked employees about what we could do better to be more customer obsessed. This generated quite a few ideas. Staff reflected that perhaps they had initially rated themselves too highly on current customer obsession. Going through the D4D process revealed an internal blind spot which had stopped us seeing all the things that we could do for our customers.'

Ben proposes that D4D is a good approach to follow for other companies because 'you only find out what you need to know by asking people about the problem.' He believes it is an easy model for people to follow. D4D only has three principles. Intuit publish these freely at www.intuitlabs.com /design-for-delight so anyone can learn more if they want to.'

CASE STUDY: AGILITY IN MIND

'Lived experience of employees is more important than written working practices.'
— Andrew Jones, CEO of Agility in Mind

Andrew describes the company as a business agility transformation consultancy, helping organisations to become more agile, flexible and responsive in the way they do things. He feels ingrained practices, processes and culture prevent organisations responding to changes in the wider environment. He aims to help people change the way they work together and get employees to feel more confident about changes they can make themselves.

In terms of diversity and inclusion, Andrew feels that organisations have reached the point where things need to adapt more rapidly. Digital engagement has forced the issue and created new expectations of employers, especially amongst younger people.

Agility in Mind gets to know the client organisation well, asking, 'What are the constraints, both real and perceived? How do people work together? What is the content of employee dialogue?' It's important to respect that each organisation is different and evolving, which builds credibility with clients and paints a clear picture of what's going on.

Things start to change when employees start to do things differently. Agility in Mind creates their impact through training and a simple toolkit, focused on people working together more effectively.

Creating an Agile and Inclusive Culture

Setting outcomes, essentially the characteristics that the organisation is trying to achieve, is vital. Andrew advocates a multi-disciplinary team approach, where the team builds a roadmap and breaks big milestones down into smaller tasks.

'We don't want the programme to be seen as just another HR initiative. Diversity and inclusion affects everyone and we don't want lip service. A multi-disciplinary team is better aligned to achieve outcomes across the whole organisation.'

Involving people across the organisation breaks down barriers and encourages adoption and when people start to see there's something in it for their team, or solves some of their problems, it creates buy-in across teams and departments.

Senior people must lead change and Agility in Mind's training instils a shared common language about the organisation: a single key person being off message can easily undo the team's work.

Benefits of Agile

Andrew contrasts Agile principles with waterfall project management. In waterfall a project team spends a lot of time documenting a plan, then works through the plan, only testing outputs near the endpoint. Progress isn't visible.

Agile is about incremental change in small steps. Tasks are completed quickly, and progress can be seen. People aren't stuck in a room writing a theoretical plan. The Agile process is iterative, providing live learning feedback throughout implementation. This way there is a better chance change will stick and become part of the culture.

Agile Principles

Agile prioritises conversations over documentation. The first item on the Agile Manifesto is 'individuals and interactions over processes and tools.' Andrew thinks that people forget that the way they work together is the most important thing. He adds, 'What tends to happen is that people look for the tangible in processes and tools and try to force those into the organisation. This approach only delivers some level of adoption. Working practices are more important than the documentation about what they are going to be. Lived experience of employees is more important than written working practices.'

Advice to HR Directors

To implement change in an Agile way, Andrew recommends that an organisation knows where it is trying to get to, getting there in small increments, a bit at a time, where you can see the benefits and learn from the process. Learning is a fundamental Agile principle.

He says, 'You won't always get it right, but it's better to find what works and what doesn't in small increments than to find a whole programme has failed.'

REFLECTION

1. How might a more human-centred approach benefit your organisation in improving its inclusive culture and infrastructure?

2. Which journeys in your organisation should you address?

3. What steps would you take to develop a more human-centred approach to implementing diversity and inclusion solutions?

In the next chapter we will talk about how technology can enable you to scale up what you are trying to achieve in diversity and inclusion.

FIVE

Cyber

The importance of technology

The use of new technology such as artificial
intelligence and machine learning, big data,
wearable tech, 5G data networks, autonomous
vehicles, blockchain and smart cities is expanding
at a vast rate. What can HR departments gain from
this technology and how can they use it to support
their organisation's diversity and inclusion strategy?
This chapter shows how technology can enhance
it. It describes systems that provide insights and
data that can help shift the culture and create those
targeted interventions where change is required. We
look at digital accessibility and assess whether your
customer-facing and internal-facing digital services
comply with requirements for all organisations to be
digitally accessible. Using the available technology
organisations can save time and money. Innovative

technology solutions are now cloud-based and easy to use.

There are many technologies available for each stage of the employee cycle. I would like to recommend software I have used when implementing diversity and inclusion strategies for various organisations.

I have grouped these technologies into four key areas:

- **Insights and data**

- **Recruitment**

- **Supporting employees**

- **Learning and development**

Insights and data

InChorus

This app allows employees to speak up about behaviours that prevent the creation of an inclusive culture. They can record examples of any micro-aggressions they have experienced or witnessed in the workplace. It then provides employers with a heat map showing where this behaviour is taking place and to which groups of people within their organisation. The app also signposts the employee to further support such as the Employee Assistance Programme, a whistle-blowing channel or the Grievance Procedure. This data allows the employer to take immediate targeted action.

Culture Amp

Culture Amp helps organisations understand their data and take appropriate action. You can conduct diversity and inclusion pulse surveys on their platform. They have an excellent reputation and it is worth browsing their website to check out how they can help enhance diversity and inclusion within your organisation.

Recruitment

Clear Talent

The Clear Talent system provides the employer with an electronic record of workplace adjustments for job candidates and employees. There are two modules – an employee module and a recruitment module. I explain the employee module under the section on Supporting Employees below. The recruitment module lets job applicants inform an organisation of any reasonable adjustments they need to take part in the recruitment process. Your recruiters can then put these reasonable adjustments in place. The software helps organise the workflow involved.

Textio

This software uses artificial intelligence and machine learning, enabling organisations to look at the language they use in job descriptions and job advertisements with the aim of getting more applicants. Textio checks the gender language used to ensure that there is a balance between masculine and feminine terminology. Otherwise an advert or job description using predominantly masculine terminology would attract more applicants with masculine characteristics and vice versa with feminine terminology. I am deliberately not saying men and women, because there are men with feminine characteristics and women with masculine characteristics; each will be attracted to the advert with terminology that resonates most with them. It scores the advertisement using a traffic-light system, looking for any elements that might dissuade people from applying. This includes the overuse of buzzwords, an advert which is too long or missing important details about the job such as flexible or agile working. It highlights areas that need to be changed to make the job advertisement or job description more effective.

Gap Jumpers

Back in the 1930s the Boston Philharmonic Orchestra was conducting a series of auditions. One of the musicians being auditioned was the nephew of the conductor. This raised concerns that he would have an unfair advantage. So, the orchestra decided to audition the musicians from behind a curtain so that the panel couldn't see who was playing. When the auditions were completed, the person who was awarded the place stepped out from behind the curtain. The panel were shocked to see that they had selected a woman. At that time, the Boston Philharmonic was an all-male orchestra. The panel had stumbled across a way of preventing unconscious bias in the auditioning process. They realised that in normal auditions they listened with their eyes, not with their ears. Rather than concentrate on the quality of the sounds produced, they looked at how the musician held their instrument, what they looked like on stage, their posture. It is ironic that though they were hiring people to play music, the quality of music turned out to be the least important aspect.

Gap Jumpers enables organisations to reduce unconscious bias from their recruitment process. At the BBC, I piloted Gap Jumpers and, just as in the Boston Philharmonic example above, conducted blind auditions. I worked with hiring managers to create an online challenge for candidates, replicating the type of tasks they might end up doing if they got the job. It was to be done at home and in their own time. Working with a BBC iPlayer hiring manager, we asked candidates to create a small, new feature for iPlayer. Applicants were asked to submit their creations to us anonymously. Gap Jumpers software checked for any plagiarism before the hiring manager assessed the quality of the submissions. His selection was therefore based on the quality of work. Only then were the CVs released to him. In piloting Gap Jumpers software, we saw an increase in the number of candidates from ethnic minority backgrounds, and female candidates, getting through to interview. This was significant given that this part of the BBC was a male-dominated technology and engineering division. Gap Jumpers also allowed us to make job offers more quickly and reduced the amount of time it took to hire new staff. Hiring managers felt that the quality of interviewed candidates improved using this software.

There were other success stories. One candidate had a severe speech impediment which became worse if he was anxious. He found telephone interviews, often the first step in the recruitment process, stressful. He frequently failed to progress to the next stage. Because we gave him the opportunity to complete a challenge at home in his own time, he proved that he had the skills to do the job. He was able to progress to the interview stage.

In effect, we turned the recruitment process upside down by giving all applicants a challenge at the beginning, rather than at the end of it.

Supporting employees

Cognisess

This system gives organisations the ability to measure cognitive diversity through gamification. By playing games, organisations can create a profile of their cognitive diversity by team. This enables them to make decisions about whether they want to hire somebody who might think differently from the rest of the team. It can be used at different stages of the employee lifecycle. At the recruitment stage, a manager might have a team profile that looks like X, but has decided they need a candidate with different characteristics if the team is to fully embrace diversity. Cognisess is featured as a case study at the end of this chapter. It goes into more depth on how the system works.

Clear Talent

This software normalises disability by providing employees with an electronic record that logs the workplace adjustments they need to remove any barriers from preventing them from doing their role. It talks about the barriers and obstacles employees face rather than their disabilities. It applies to all groups that require adjustments. This includes working parents, those with fluctuating health conditions, employees who have a caring role: anyone who might need flexible working arrangements or other workplace adjustments. This triggers a workflow that starts with a conversation between the employee and their manager, who then involves the appropriate departments to fulfil the employee's requirements. System reports show what adjustments are requested across the organisation, at what cost, and how long it takes to fulfil requests.

Learning and development

Crescendo

This young start-up company is one to watch. Their software injects diversity and inclusion training and knowledge in a bite-sized way into the collaboration platform, Slack. Based on the employees' responses, it tweaks the content that it generates. It understands an employee's level of awareness and understanding. An advanced user who knows a lot about diversity and inclusion will get different content to a beginner. Diversity and inclusion training is costly because it is classroom-based learning. Some organisations provide digital courses delivered on their own learning management system, but these are expensive to produce and need regular updating. Crescendo avoids these problems by being nimble, agile and using Slack (which many organisations use) as the learning platform.

Learning and development is an expanding area. I know one company that uses virtual reality to teach about micro-aggressions. The employee puts on a headset and finds themselves in a meeting with two male colleagues. The employee, as the user of the system, is the female colleague. Each time they think they experience a micro-aggression, they hit a virtual button. Because of the total immersion, employees find this an excellent way of learning. This piece of software is currently in research and development. Early signs show that it is producing increased levels of emotional intelligence in the user.

Digital Accessibility

Digital accessibility is crucial if an organisation is to fully embrace diversity and inclusion. Organisations don't give enough consideration as to whether their customer-facing digital products (their website or app), or internal-facing systems (intranet or learning management system), are accessible to everyone. Is their learning management system accessible to people with sight loss or a hearing impairment? Are training videos subtitled? What about those who have difficulty using a mouse? How accessible is your website? Does it adhere to Web Content Accessibility Guidelines (WCAG) standards? Does it meet international standards like ISO 30071–1?[1] This is a code of practice for creating accessible

---

1   ISO 30071–1 Information technology – Development of user interface accessibility – Part 1: Code of practice for creating accessible ICT products and services, www.iso.org/standard/70913.html

ICT (information and communications technology) products and services.

It is vital that organisations address this and make the necessary changes to correct and improve digital accessibility. There are four key reasons why this is so important:

1. The Legal case

Organisations are at risk of litigation if they do not ensure that their digital systems are accessible. We see this particularly in the US where many organisations are being challenged and taken to court by disability campaign organisations over the inaccessibility of their products and services. In the UK we are governed by the Equality Act 2010 which states that organisations must ensure accessibility to their products and services.

2. The Financial case

Servicing people online (essentially self-service) is cheaper than them visiting a branch or phoning a call centre. HR departments have found that it is far less expensive to have employees self-serve through an online portal than having a staffed internal HR helpdesk.

3. The Ethical case

It is inappropriate and unethical for organisations to talk publicly about how inclusive they are when their digital technology is not accessible.

4. The Innovation case

Much of today's technology was created for people with various disabilities. Text messaging was apparently created to help deaf people communicate. Now nearly everybody texts.

Everybody benefits from Assistive Technology

When we talk about accessibility, it's not just for people with permanent disabilities like mine. I have a genetic neuromuscular disability that I was born with called Spinal Muscular Atrophy. It means that all my muscles are very weak. I use speech-to-text software on my laptop. I also have Siri to help me with phoning. And I use Amazon Echo in my home to control the thermostat and lights.

People can also be 'impaired' situationally. Let's say your hands are busy while cooking so you use voice recognition technology. Or someone might be temporarily impaired with a broken arm and have difficulty typing. Organisations must recognise that digital accessibility is not just for people with permanent conditions, it should include technology for temporary and situationally impaired people. Examples of assistive technologies are the speech-to-text software, Dragon Naturally Speaking; Read & Write Gold for dyslexic people; screen readers such as JAWS for visually-impaired people. They also need to think about hardware: ergonomic mice for anyone with difficulty using a regular mouse, mini keyboards rather than regular-sized keyboards. I recommend that organisations keep an up-to-date catalogue of the most commonly used assistive technology software with licences readily available so that your IT help desk can install it as soon as it is required.

I spent many years working in usability and accessibility at the BBC, but I am not an expert in digital accessibility. If you want to explore this issue further, visit Hassell Inclusion's website who are the UK's leading experts in digital accessibility.[2] They can carry out an audit of how accessible your digital

---

2   Hassell Inclusion, www.hassellinclusion.com

products are, provide training for your software developers, designers or product managers, and look at the governance of accessibility in your organisation.

The dark side of technology

Not all technology is helpful for diversity and inclusion. There have been news stories over the last few years about robots and Artificial Intelligence behaving badly and causing havoc in an organisation. Amazon found themselves in a difficult position when they discovered that their recruitment process had become sexist by screening out potential female candidates. Investigation revealed that the artificial intelligence software used in the selection process had been created by an all-male team and had adopted their biases. A report by James Cook published in 2019 in *The Telegraph* revealed a 'racist' passport photo system.[3] It had rejected the image of a young black man despite its meeting government standards. This was embarrassing for the UK government who had not tested the software

3   Cook, J (2019), '"Racist" passport photo system rejects image of a young black man despite meeting government standards', *The Telegraph*, www.telegraph.co.uk/technology/2019/09/19/racist-passport-photo-system-rejects-image-young-black-man-despite

thoroughly. The software 'thought' that the applicant had his mouth open in the photo. On the feedback form, the applicant wrote 'My mouth is closed, I just have big lips.' The press picked up the story after he posted it online. When creating software, we must be conscious of any bias that might go into its development. However, I am a lot more hopeful about the opportunities that software does offer for organisations to scale up their diversity and inclusion.

The future for digital services

Digital services are constantly improving. The future is full of opportunities for organisations to consider how they can take advantage of them to improve diversity and inclusion. The following advances look particularly exciting:

- **TENGAI** is an AI robot developed with a Swedish recruitment agency to eliminate bias in the recruitment process. This robot could be a good technology solution to removing bias at the interview stage.

- **Ory Lab Inc** is a Japanese company that is showing how disabled people can work as 'baristas'. Japan is increasingly using robots. This means that a paralysed person using a computer can instruct the robot to prepare and deliver the coffee to the customer, all from their own bed. This could be an innovative way of getting disabled people into employment.

I believe the future of diversity and inclusion, combined with technology, has phenomenal potential for the future. Artificial intelligence, machine learning and robotics can radically change the inclusivity of organisations provided they embrace the possibilities and the opportunities technology presents. My advice is not to wait any longer.

CASE STUDY: DATA CAN ANSWER BIG QUESTIONS

What is Cognisess?

Cognisess is a software platform that produces predictive people analytics, providing organisations with the right information to develop a high-performance workforce. Its end-to-end employee lifecycle solutions optimise the potential of the talent pool and supports retention. CEO, Chris Butt, describes the software as an enabler allowing businesses to 'better understand their talent potential' and giving individuals 'an insight into who they really are'. Chris expresses a desire to democratise human capital, believing it should be the first thing that leaders look at on the company's balance sheet.

Start with the data

Dr Boris Altemeyer, the company's Chief Scientific Officer, leads on the system's psychology and neuroscience which give individuals equal chances to show what they can do. The technology produces objective metrics that support unbiased decision-making. Data collection uses gamification of information processing and decision-making activities, a strategy aimed to put people at ease.

The platform measures fit for team and culture, with activities that involve prioritising or sacrificing values. The algorithm works out their abilities and values in the background. Employers often focus on where a candidate rates highest, but Boris recommends analysing what their trade-offs were. Was it supporting others or achievement and recognition that was the first to go under pressure? Through data, Cognisess aims to mitigate the variability of human interpretation, neutralising notions of culture and team fit gathered from curriculum vitae and job interviews alone.

Interrogating the data: creating a different conversation

With Cognisess data, leaders can ask the system a range of questions to improve business performance. Leaders can plot out and visualise how people are thinking and see in which areas they might differ or are the same. Alignment across teams and culture is visualised over multiple domains, to see where a team is stretched. Individuals are represented anonymously, by dots on a screen. Fit is always determined by the company's own proposed values.

Cognisess data can answer key questions: do we have enough leaders, problem solvers and planners? Inevitably there will be variables outside the raw data, but the data can be the starting point. Cognisess can be used to quickly formulate teams and offset expedience and similarity bias. If a team is too streamlined, it can lead to communication issues. Visualisations of teams that might have a propensity for groupthink and could struggle with solving wicked problems is powerful. The data informs team reconfiguration prioritising diversity of thinking. Using this data-led approach, recruitment practices become more inclusive and objective.

Changing the culture: how business can hardwire diversity and inclusion in their DNA

Cognisess is non-prescriptive and can be used as an 'out of the box' or as a highly bespoke solution. It can 'hold the mirror up' as companies clarify their cultural values in relation to the values of candidates and employees. It's always down to the companies to decide their values, Cognisess helps to visualise them.

Cognisess wants data to be accessible and transparent, to inform operations. They believe data can answer big questions such as, 'Do we have enough cognitive diversity in the team?' Since people can get fixed in their ways, the platform gives organisations the option to get the data to do some of the work of driving change. Cognisess emphasises that the platform works best with the human decision-making element, which is more sensitive to factors like context.

Cognisess can get diversity through the door and create a more inclusive culture.

The platform supports talent attraction and screening, allowing hirers to be blind to factors other than how candidates think, their talent potential and where they would fit. If an organisation truly commits to developing inclusion and diversity in its workforce Cognisess can accelerate that process.

CASE STUDY: INCHORUS

'Without data it's hard for organisations to
know where to focus efforts to build inclusivity.'
— Raj Ramanandi and Rosie Turner,
founders of InChorus

InChorus uses technology to 'shine a light on
bias to grow an inclusive organisation'. Previous
experience in an HR tech company developed
Rosie's interest in technology apps making better
workplaces. Diversity and inclusion formed a key
area of her work, understanding the challenges
and looking at existing technological solutions.

Raj has start-up entrepreneurship and venture
capital experience but found it unrewarding to
'teach rich companies how to make more money'.

Improving an Organisation's Diversity and Inclusion

InChorus works at an organisational and employee
level. From an organisation's perspective, it's
beneficial when employees can share problems
before they become too big. Data collection
enables organisations to pinpoint potential
issues and analyse any relationships to workforce
demographics. Without data it's hard for

organisations to know where to focus efforts to build inclusivity, meaning interventions can become random or ineffective.

How Does InChorus Work?

InChorus fits into the workplace toolkit, between employee surveys and whistleblowing policies. The InChorus app captures employees' subjective experience of everyday incidents like bias, micro-aggressions, or bullying and harassment. Employees access the app through a login. It typically takes an employee between 45–60 secs to log any incident in detail. The logging process itself provides employee validation. The app also gives individuals access to specific resources. These could be educational, and self-help related, or signpost to more information internally or externally.

The app operates an incident typology, prompting the user to pick as many as are relevant. Different interactions are captured: non-verbal, gestural and verbal. The employee also logs whether they feel the incident is linked to any aspects of their identity. InChorus links these incidents to any protected characteristics the employee identifies.

The HR dashboard then anonymises and aggregates the workforce data collected through the app. This allows the organisation to see what is happening, where and when. Trends can be identified and measured to see if resulting actions taken are improving inclusion.

Reasons to Adopt

Some clients may not have specific problems in their organisations, but adopting the platform demonstrates concern for employees, fostering goodwill and wellbeing. Other clients need reliable information to analyse existing problems, eg the annual employee survey tells them the company struggles to move the needle on bullying.

InChorus captures insights and clarifies data around micro-aggression and bias.

Knowing the types of incidents and where in the organisation they occur means action can be targeted. Allocating resources to interventions becomes more effective because the organisation sees exactly what and where the problem is. Turning a hunch into datasets allows HR to take the evidence to senior management and mirrors how other parts of the business work. Diversity and inclusion should be the same.

Workplace Culture

InChorus links everything back to workplace culture by embedding employee voice and feedback. Data helps predict where within the business problems are most likely to arise.

Businesses can then react swiftly, formulate actions and shift the culture, particularly workplace bias which InChorus feels is a neglected area.

REFLECTION

1. If your organisation invested in research and development of future technologies, how could this make your workplace more inclusive?

2. By increasing the use of technology for diversity and inclusion, what could you achieve in your organisation?

3. How accessible are your internally- and externally-facing digital products and services?

In the next chapter we will be discussing how the whole of the organisation needs to take responsibility for diversity and inclusion and that this is not just a matter for the HR team.

SIX

Collaboration

The key message of both this chapter and book is that diversity and inclusion is everybody's responsibility, not just the HR department's, which is so often the case. When asked who is responsible for diversity and inclusion in an organisation, my reply is that it's often left with the HR department because it seems like a natural fit given that diversity and inclusion is largely about the workforce and people.

But there are issues with this attitude. I work with many senior people and I find that those in the C-Suite don't take enough personal responsibility and accountability for diversity and inclusion. It is often delegated to an HR Director or to a Head of Diversity and Inclusion. Without Chief Executive and Board level support, many of my clients struggle to implement significant diversity and inclusion because they lack top-level sponsorship. While the Chief Executive Officer (CEO) should ultimately be accountable, responsibility should sit with the whole of the C-suite. And if I had to pick one individual on the Board responsible for diversity and inclusion, it would be the Chief Operating Officer (COO). They are in charge of the efficient running of the organisation and can establish an overarching strategy that is clear and easy for people to understand and which every department can own and implement.

The strategy acts as an umbrella across the whole organisation into which each department will feed its own set of objectives and targets. Departments have their own unique challenges and nuances that should be addressed on a more local level. For example:

- Technology departments may have issues with gender imbalance. The engineering and tech space tends to be male dominated and may require specific activity around gender balance and digital accessibility.

- Research and development departments can leverage diversity to increase their level of innovation. The more diverse teams are, the more cutting edge and better at problem-solving. This can lead to new products, services and markets.

- Customer-facing or customer service teams need to be able to empathise and respond to a diverse customer base. They would benefit from increasing their Cultural Intelligence (CQ) scores.

- The HR team has to ensure that all their processes, from recruitment and onboarding to performance and development, are as inclusive as possible. Everyone should be able to progress in the organisation on equal terms.

- A diverse supply chain and a fair, transparent procurement process come under the remit of the Procurement department. This creates a level playing field for your suppliers. Procurement should consider suppliers owned by minority groups or run by female chief executives. The procurement team should ask suppliers how they'll deliver diversity themselves.

- The Marketing department should be mindful that their campaigns reflect the diversity of the customers that their business serves.

- Internal Communications teams should be rigorous about the language and images they use.

- Other teams and departments also have a role in creating a more diverse and inclusive business.

Everyone has a part to play. This means employees, leaders, teams, suppliers, strategic partners, clients and outside organisations must work together. Collaboration is vital to implementing your diversity and inclusion strategy. And to have a full impact, it has to reach beyond the confines of your own organisation. This includes:

- Global and local implementation of the strategy

- Communication with all employees

- Involvement of all employee resource groups or diversity networks

- Involvement of customers

- Building a diverse supply chain

- Forming industry alliances

- Including shareholders

- Including the local community in which you operate

By working collaboratively, you reduce the risk of silo working, you encourage broader thinking and more creative problem-solving. Diversity and inclusion won't be just an internal issue but will reach a wider spectrum of different industries, both nationally and globally.

The Global Plan

Collaboration goes beyond the internal workings of an organisation. It's about thinking globally but acting locally. I work with several businesses with offices all over the world and employing thousands of people. I also work with organisations with one or two offices in the UK. I give the same advice to both – take a global approach to designing your diversity and inclusion strategy. But when it comes to delivering it, think locally. Local differences need to be taken account of. An office in London will have differing needs to an office in Sheffield, even if they are both part of the same organisation. Think of the differences between a London base and ones in Los Angeles or Bangalore. You might have an overarching strategy for diversity and inclusion for the whole organisation, but without taking into account the local situation, it won't be effective.

When organisations launch their strategy and talk about it publicly, they should be prepared for a backlash. Open support of the rights of LGBT+ individuals might cause problems in markets where being gay is unlawful. A global organisation has to stand up for what they believe in and develop a local response. Vodafone has made a global commitment to LGBT+ equality. A Stonewall Report entitled

'Safe Travels – Global Mobility for LGBT Staff' featured Vodafone as a case study. It highlighted a project supporting LGBT+ employees travelling internationally with the company.[1] Vodafone created a toolkit for HR professionals and line managers, together with advice and support, for employees travelling to high risk areas in the world.

Organisations with offices in several countries may find a difference in how advanced diversity and inclusion is in each location. It is usually well implemented when the local leadership takes personal responsibility and accountability for diversity and inclusion in that region. Variation between countries can occur if the global CEO does not take responsibility for global oversight.

The global CEO needs an overall perspective to ensure consistency across the whole of the organisation. If the organisation has offices in the UK and India then the global strategy for diversity and inclusion should apply to both countries, while taking into account local nuances. There should also be adequate funding and resources. I work with some organisations who have a team in one country with a good budget for diversity and inclusion.

---

1   Stonewall, 'Safe Travels – Global Mobility for LGBT Staff', www
     .equality.admin.cam.ac.uk/files/stonewall_-_safe_travels_guide.pdf

Teams in other countries are expected to do it on a shoestring with no dedicated staff. Regional offices should also be accountable for implementing diversity and inclusion and not be allowed to get away with doing nothing or the bare minimum. They need to deliver sustainable change.

The key message is that organisations need to take a global position but act locally. It is the global CEO, rather than the country's or region's CEO, who is accountable for the diversity and inclusion strategy. This ensures consistency across the whole organisation. There should be regional plans that feed into the overarching global strategy. These should be budgeted and resourced adequately, with everyone being held accountable.

Everyone has a role to play

Including all employees in the delivery of your diversity and inclusion strategy is challenging. Without this involvement, you might find that the only people interested in implementing the strategy are those with a personal interest. Perhaps they are from a minority group or have a personal connection. The challenge is to reach beyond individual groups and capture the interest of all employees

regardless of their backgrounds and beliefs. You
want to increase collaboration and connection across
minority groups so that inclusion extends beyond
the silos that can be unconsciously created by the
groups themselves.

Key to this is increasing the visibility of diversity and
inclusion. There are several ways to do this:

- Instigate conversations throughout the
  organisation wherever and whenever possible.

- Ensure frequent internal communications from
  the CEO and senior leadership team.

- Position signs and symbols around the building
  to remind people of diversity and inclusion.
  Why not give lanyards to everyone in support
  of diversity and inclusion or have merchandise
  around the office such as mouse mats, mugs and
  pens? Place thought-provoking posters in your
  lifts and where people make their coffee. Don't
  underestimate the power of these small actions.
  Remember the employee who felt able to come
  out in the workplace when he saw his boss
  carrying a mug inscribed *'I'm an LGBT+ ally'*?

These techniques will increasingly bring diversity
and inclusion into the everyday vocabulary of

employees so that it becomes part of the daily conversation.

It is crucial that organisations make it clear to their employees that everyone is responsible for diversity and inclusion and their behaviours regarding it. Any inappropriate behaviours will carry consequences. List the behaviours you expect when you define the culture you want. This starts with the management and senior leadership team. How *they* behave and act as role models will cascade through the organisation. In my interview with Emma Codd from Deloitte, she explains the importance of having a Leadership Charter which outlines the behaviours expected from leaders in the company. This is something other organisations might wish to replicate.

Your values also need to align with your diversity and inclusion strategy. There is no point claiming organisational values if no-one upholds them. One organisation I worked with displayed the values of the organisation on the wall of the lobby for everyone to see. Although diversity was included in their values, the employees I was training didn't agree. They felt the company didn't really embrace diversity and that the CEO seemed not to care about it. When diversity was clearly displayed as a value, why wasn't the organisation living and breathing diversity? Organisations have a responsibility to breathe life into their values, from the CEO to the newly appointed apprentice. It applies to all employees, not just those from a minority background or those with a personal interest (perhaps their son or daughter has autism and they are interested in neurodiversity within the organisation).

Employee networks

Employee networks or employee resource groups (ERGs) are key in implementing diversity and inclusion in large organisations. Networks such as the Women's Network, Gender Network, Black, Asian and Minority Ethnic (BAME) Network, Disability Network, Muslim, Christian or Jewish Networks can help implement change at grassroots level. They bring people together, raise awareness from the events they organise, and get feedback from employees about what it is like working within the organisation.

They also come with flaws. I often find that they are not strategically aligned with the organisation's diversity and inclusion strategy. They often do their own thing or create something which is contrary to the central strategy. Alignment is vital if a central strategy is to be implemented across the organisation.

Networks often lack resources in terms of time, people and money. Without an adequate budget it is difficult to do anything effective. People are expected to run the network in addition to their day job. If you work in an organisation where one of your key performance measures is your billability, volunteering to run a network will reduce your billable hours and won't be fully supported by the business. Think about how you recognise and reward network leaders who are delivering great value to the culture of the organisation.

Network groups might not always be run properly. They often lack Terms of Reference or the right decision makers around the table. To ensure networks run effectively, you need a Chair, a Treasurer and a Project Manager at the very least. It should be run like a proper committee.

They also tend to attract only people affiliated to the topic, rather than a broad spectrum of people. The Women's Network will predominantly attract women. The Muslim Network will have mainly Muslim members. If we want to increase diversity and inclusion in organisations, everybody must be part of the conversation. Men need to be part of the

Women's Network, non-Muslim colleagues part
of the Muslim network, non-disabled members of
the disability network, etc. This demonstrates true
inclusion across these networks. One way to do this
is by creating allies in a systematic and organised
way. The LGBT+ Network might actively recruit
allies to support the network who may not be
LGBT+ themselves, but who publicly support the
work the network does. For it to work, you must
define what an ally is and what is involved in the
role. Do they need to attend quarterly meetings
and commit to a set of actions? How do you recruit
them? How do you inform the organisation who
your allies are? Correctly implemented, it prevents
networks working in silos, which is a key issue.
Collaboration can play an important part in this. An
Inclusion Council could bring the Chairs of all the
network groups together on a regular basis. In this
way diverse networks can meet regularly to share
common issues and tackle problems.

At one organisation I worked with, we were building
a new head office. I met with our LGBT+ Network
to discuss gender neutral toilets. Then I realised I
needed to meet the Disability Network regarding
accessible toilets. And the Muslim Network needed
to be consulted about washing facilities prior to
prayer. In effect, the conversation on toilets involved
not one but three very different networks. It's

why collaboration across networks is important.
Otherwise it's difficult to understand and appreciate
the needs of individual groups. Network groups can
influence the acceptance of diversity and inclusion as
the organisation grows.

Involving customers

Diversity and inclusion can be quite inward-looking,
focusing mainly on the workforce. Collaboration
with customers means that the strategy can also
reflect their needs. You can include customers by
carrying out research. My favoured approach to this
is ethnographic research which allows you to create
authentic human stories. Organisations usually
identify general personas for customers. Joe Bloggs,
for example, works in a generic career in a generic
city. If you use an actual person, a named individual,
this has a much greater impact. Take me as an
example of a customer. You might say the following:

> 'One of our customers is called Toby. He
> lives with his partner in London. He loves
> watching Netflix in the evening. He goes
> around in a wheelchair and has a warped
> sense of humour.'

If you can create a personal story around an individual, and bring them to life in the organisation, they can be used as an avatar for employees to help them connect with their customers.

Involving your supply chain

Your supply chain can often be overlooked when it comes to diversity and inclusion. As well as employees and customers, organisations also need to focus on their supply chain. This includes strategic partners such as the companies you outsource to, so that they can help you achieve your diversity and inclusion objectives. They also have to be diverse. And it works both ways. When I worked at a consultancy firm, the security and front-of-house staff were outsourced to another company. They were fantastic colleagues: inclusive, welcoming and warm. One security guard I got to know was an aspiring technologist. She was doing this job during the day and attending night classes in the evening. I wondered whether there was any potential for my organisation to partner with the outsourced company. If one of their security guards was training to be a technologist, why shouldn't we support them? Perhaps my organisation could offer them work experience? Or contribute towards their education?

Or put them on a training programme once they had
their college qualification? My employer already
had a relationship with this company and their
staff were aware of the culture of my organisation.
It seemed like a natural fit to me. Many of the
front-of-house people were from an ethnic minority
background. It could be a good opportunity to get
more diversity into the professional services industry
by encouraging lateral moves and promoting social
mobility.

You need to provide the companies in your supply
chain with a statement on diversity and inclusion.
You must demonstrate a fair and transparent process
when it comes to selecting suppliers. Organisations
often produce statements on anti-slavery, fair trade,
sustainability or eco sustainability. When it comes to
procurement, they often omit to include anything on
diversity.

Industry alliances

Many organisations are inward-looking when it
comes to diversity and inclusion. They hold their
cards close to their chests and are reluctant to work
together in case any of their flaws or weaknesses
are exposed. Diversity and inclusion does give

an organisation a competitive advantage, but equally they need to work together to improve it across all industries. Each sector will throw up its own diversity and inclusion challenges. If you take technology, science or engineering, it's predominantly the gender imbalance issue. It makes sense for companies in the STEM (science, technology, engineering and mathematics) sector to work together to address the gender problem. City and finance businesses often have issues around agile and flexible working. The TV and film industry has issues around the portrayal of people from ethnic minority backgrounds. Industry specific issues are better tackled in conjunction with other organisations in the same sector. Working as a collective to come up with solutions.

Many organisations are proactive and have already started to create associations. The Tech Talent Charter, as a case in point, is sponsored by the Department for Media, Sports and Culture. Organisations can also get together across different sectors. This has the potential to create some innovative solutions. What would happen if a shipping freight company got together with a bath soap manufacturer? What could these intersections bring to diversity and inclusion? They might create unique perspectives and solutions to tackling diversity and inclusion for the whole country.

Shareholders

Shareholders also have a role to play in an organisation's diversity and inclusion strategy. The synergy between the shareholder and the organisation is clear. Organisations create value for shareholders. Shareholders will benefit from taking an active interest in diversity and inclusion and should hold the CEO and the leadership team accountable. Not only does diversity and inclusion improve the performance of a business, it is important for the future of the organisation. It future proofs the organisation by making it sustainable, resilient and allows it to flourish. It taps into new markets. It allows organisations to innovate, create, improve retention and reduce attrition. Shareholders have a significant vested interest in all these aspects and therefore have a key role in making this happen.

In summary, collaboration internally and externally is vital to ensure the proper implementation of your diversity and inclusion strategy. Central to this are the following:

- Global and local implementation of the diversity and inclusion strategy
- Communication with all employees

- Involvement of all Employee Network groups

- Involvement of customers

- Building a diverse supply chain

- Forming industry alliances

- Including shareholders

CASE STUDY: HIGH SPEED 2 (HS2)

'Accountability from the top and participation from the ground.'
— Mark Lomas, Head of Equality, Diversity and Inclusion (EDI) for High Speed 2

HS2 is a high-speed railway construction project that will connect the cities of London, Birmingham, Manchester and Leeds. It is Europe's largest infrastructure project.

Mark's team sits in the HR Directorate. The team deliver on internal and supply chain equality, diversity and inclusion performance, communities and engagement and HS2 train and station design.

Supply Chain Diversity: UK leading

Mark thinks HS2 has a UK leading approach 'because our award-winning Inclusive Procurement model is end-to-end. It's baked in at every stage of the procurement process along with effective monitoring. This applies to small and multi-billion-pound contracts.

Organisations often confuse inclusive procurement with supplier diversity. The two are different. We have an inclusive procurement model which incorporates both. Inclusive procurement is how you measure diversity and inclusion within the procurement approach. Then there is the measurement of diversity within the supply chain.'

Assets and Built Environment

Mark knows it's hard to retrofit large infrastructure projects. 'That's why we need diverse perspectives.'

HS2 involve customers in design through a customer panel. The panel is made up of a diverse group of people who test ideas. There is also a regular online forum. Panel members also get together a couple of times a year for deep-dive discussions. HS2 share a built environment accessibility panel (BEAP) with Network Rail who work to provide in-depth reviews on the accessibility features of designs.

Aligning Outsourcing Partners

Mark explains how HS2 have got their suppliers on board with equality, diversity and inclusion, so it's not just about paying lip service. He says 'This is a stone-cold business case. Potential suppliers can win or lose business because of their performance on EDI and skills, employment and education. On a commercial tender, the win or lose margin can be a 3% difference or even smaller.'

The HS2 approach is starting to influence the wider sector. There is a move towards a uniform method of sector-wide EDI reporting this year, aligned with HS2 reporting. Mark knows it's different in terms of the scale of influence for a large company like HS2, but he believes other sectors can also change through corporate expectations.

Staff Networks

A fifth of HS2 staff is involved in diversity networks.

'The networks are set four challenges that align with the HS2 EDI Strategy goals. Networks can only access funding by showing alignment with those goals. Through working on the shared challenges, the networks connect. Collaboration is encouraged, but I remain to be convinced that one overarching inclusion network is the way to go. Additionally, separate networks can end up talking to themselves in an echo chamber.'

He summarises the dilemma. 'It's obvious there are organic opportunities to collaborate as well as to do things separately. The allies model works very well. HS2 have a gender balance network and multicultural network.'

Setting Expectations of Staff

HS2 have implemented a two-fold process of expectation setting. Mark explains, 'There is accountability from the top and participation from the ground up. EDI participation expectations are in everyone's objectives.

The Senior Leadership Team have specific performance indicators linked to end of year performance. The CEO sets the expectation on leaders regarding EDI.'

Leaders are accountable for ensuring people in their directorate complete all mandatory EDI training and that everyone has participated in one EDI event in the year. They are also accountable for meeting the expectation for their participation in events and programmes.

Leadership Framework

The HS2 Leadership Framework embeds specific EDI indicators through its competency structures. These cover areas such as including innovation, collaboration, growing talent and inspirational leadership. This was the culmination of HR teams working together lead by Organisational Development and Change team.

Mark outlines the expectation. 'We assess employee development needs against the framework. This informs their professional development plan. We recruit senior leaders against the framework. That's how HS2 permeates equality, diversity and inclusion through leadership structures. It's built into performance development, competence and recruitment.' To achieve this the whole HR function needs to collaborate.

REFLECTION

1. How invested is your Chief Executive Officer in diversity and inclusion?

2. What would it take for your CEO to be more accountable and responsible for diversity and inclusion across the whole of the business globally? And global could mean your offices in the UK or across the world.

3. How are you increasing the dialogue on diversity and inclusion within the entire organisation so that every single employee understands what it's about and proactively wants to get involved?

4. How are you thinking beyond the organisation and involving people outside of your business, including customers, suppliers, strategic partners and other organisations in your industry?

5. How do you encourage your shareholders to take an active interest in diversity and inclusion and hold the business accountable for making positive changes in diversity and inclusion?

In the next chapter we will talk about how to increase your profile as an inclusive employer and employer of choice.

SEVEN

Celebration

Why celebrate at the end?

This chapter is about celebration. It is slightly tongue-in-cheek to have it at the end of my Inclusive Growth System but that is because so many organisations do the awards and the celebrations at the beginning of their diversity and inclusion strategy process.

Often the day-to-day experience of the employees doesn't match the image an organisation presents to the world. Despite companies appearing in the press for winning awards for inclusivity, it's not the culture employees encounter when they go to work. They don't feel like they belong, or that they are in a particularly inclusive workplace. Managers could be guilty of spending more time filling in award entries rather than making systemic change to make their organisation more inclusive. To prevent this happening, organisations need to undertake the work described in the preceding chapters before they even begin to celebrate. When they reach this chapter, it's time to create a plan. A strategic and structured roadmap that leads to celebration that promotes their employer brand.

Many awards and benchmarks don't result in creating inclusive cultures. I suspect some are more about the commercial viability of hosting the awards and the ego of the organisers. Awards ought to result in raising the profile of the organisation. Unfortunately, it's often not the case. For that reason, it's important to be selective about which awards and benchmarks you go for. What is important is not so much the award as whether your organisation is seen as an inclusive employer.

What is celebration about?

Celebration is about achieving congruency between what you state to the market about diversity and inclusion in your organisation and the day-to-day experience of your employees. The aims of celebrating as an organisation are to:

- Amplify your message and make sure the right people hear it.

- Increase your profile as an inclusive employer.

- Position your organisation as an employer of choice so that you attract the best talent.

- Increase your employees' sense of pride in the organisation so you retain them and increase their level of engagement.

The key message in this chapter is not to spend a lot of time, effort and energy entering awards unless they fulfil these criteria. Otherwise they are just a quick win that looks good on paper or on your website. In reality, they won't make a profound impact on your organisation.

Ways to increase organisational profile

There are many ways to raise the profile of your organisation other than awards. The following is not an exhaustive list, but may help you think of other ways to become known as an inclusive employer.

Social media

Social media platforms are key when promoting your organisation. I advise all organisations I work with to start with a listening exercise on social media channels. You can commission an agency to do this, or you can do it in-house. Audit what people say about diversity and inclusion in your organisation on the major social media platforms such as LinkedIn, Twitter, Instagram and Facebook. Then take account of the less obvious ones such as Glassdoor and Indeed.

Be strategic and proactive in your interactions and don't allow your organisation to become reactive. Create a calendar of events and key messages to run over the coming months or year. Build your social media campaign around these occasions. Focus on the platforms that are most relevant for your organisation. Does your audience spend most of its time on LinkedIn? If that is the case, then concentrate on creating content for LinkedIn, but be sure to replicate that content on other platforms such as Twitter, Instagram, Facebook or Glassdoor.

Job websites

Organisations underestimate the significance of job websites at their peril. There are two I want to mention – Glassdoor and Indeed. These are important because employees can leave reviews about the organisations they work for – positive and negative. If current or former employees post negative messages, this damages your employer brand because prospective employees research these websites when applying for jobs. They can see if your organisation is not an inclusive employer, or if the culture is not good to work in. I have used Glassdoor in the past to research what other disabled people say about an organisation I would like to apply for. I have accepted and rejected job offers depending on what I have read about them. It is vital, therefore, to review what is being posted about your organisation. Glassdoor also works with employers by providing a range of products and services they can use to enhance their brands on their platform.

Awards and benchmarks

Having suggested that most awards and benchmarks aren't worth applying for, I am now suggesting that they can help raise your profile as an inclusive employer. You just need to be strategic about which awards you go for. When I worked as an in-house diversity and inclusion manager, I was invited to submit entries for awards and benchmarks on a weekly basis. But time spent working on awards meant less time working on initiatives that would actually change the culture of inclusivity in the organisation. In the end, I had to be strategic. I only submitted for awards that would have maximum impact on my organisation.

Having said that, some benchmarks were extremely useful exercises for benchmarking our data and employment policies. Particularly helpful were the Working Families Index, the Stonewall Equality Index and the Business Disability Forum Smart Disability benchmark. Each has an award ceremony with good press and social media coverage that helps raise the profile of shortlisted organisations.

While deciding which awards to apply for, create a calendar listing them over the whole year. There is an award season, but it's better to have events spread evenly over twelve months. By keeping a plan you know when the awards are due and what the deadlines are for submission. It also means that you can effectively resource the award entries and not over commit. Before you attend an award ceremony spend time working on your communications. Prepare a press release that can be sent as soon as the awards are announced. Make sure that you've got your social media messages ready to post, and that they have been approved internally. Doing this in advance will ensure that your communications amplify your message and contribute towards raising the profile of your organisation at the event.

Blogs

These are an excellent way to promote your organisation as an inclusive employer. The benefit is that you have editorial control. If the blog is on your website, it can help your Google juice – your Google rankings. You can link your blogs about diversity and inclusion from your careers pages to your social media channels. If you write a blog that is particularly good and topical, it might be picked up by the press. For example, a blog talking about the gender pay gap from a slightly different angle might interest the press. If they do publish it, it will raise your organisations' profile.

Industry publications

Each industry has its own leading publications whether digital or printed. Aim to get articles about the diversity and inclusion of your organisation into these publications. Anyone interested in working in your industry will be reading them. It is about positioning yourself as a leading inclusive employer in that sector. These niche publications allow you to reach your target talent.

Traditional press

Identify the key influencers in your organisation who could comment on diversity and inclusion on TV, radio or in the newspapers. They are likely to be the CEO, HR Director or someone who can talk with authority on issues related to diversity and inclusion. Some awards include the opportunity to feature in the press as part of the winning prize. If your organisation features in *The Times* Top 50 Employers for Women awards, it will have a huge impact on your profile.

Events

Don't underestimate how useful it is to attend employer, industry and university events. If you are in the tech sector you might consider the annual Silicon Milkroundabout in London. You can also find relevant meetings and network groups on Meetup. com and Eventbrite which has information about a huge range of events. Be careful to do your research first. Many of these meetings can be informal and are unlikely to appreciate you turning up with promotional banners. However, if you empower your employees to go to these groups, make sure that they take key messages or calls to action. They should invite anyone interested in working for your organisation to visit the organisation's careers site. Employees can represent your brand, talent-spot and encourage people to apply for vacancies in your organisation.

Open days are also effective. I used this strategy at the BBC when we were on a drive to get more women into technology. The BBC wasn't seen as an employer of choice in the technology world. Facebook, Google and Amazon were the preferred option. The BBC is generally viewed as employers of TV presenters, producers and journalists. But behind the scenes, the BBC employs an army of software engineers, designers, architects, project and product managers. To showcase these professions we decided to organise quarterly open days which were aimed at women. At each session we ran a series of masterclasses where attendees could learn about the BBC's cutting-edge technology. This included flagship products such as BBC iPlayer and the BBC News website, as well as what was happening in research and development. We created a marketplace where attendees could mingle with hiring managers and recruiters to find out more about what jobs were available, which they could then apply for. We were able to dispel any myths about working for the BBC. One woman thought the people working in the technology department wore smoking jackets and puffed on cigars. It was only from attending an event like this that she realised that the culture within the organisation would suit her work-life balance and allow her to work on cutting-edge products, technologies and developments.

Partnerships

Organisations need to consider who they align themselves with so that their brand is enhanced through the relationship. Recruitment agencies are the classic partnership. It is important for the agency to be on-message about your organisation's diversity and inclusion strategy. This means that when they shortlist applicants on your behalf you receive a diverse selection of candidates.

Brand sponsorship is another form of partnership. Any organisation you work with needs to reflect your diversity, values and inclusivity.

Campaign management

I've shared several ways that organisations can increase their profile as an inclusive employer, but there are many more options. The important thing is to implement your plan in a structured and organised fashion. I recommend taking a campaign approach to promoting your organisation. This will prevent you from being disorganised, sporadic and reactive.

Before you begin to create a campaign, ask yourself these six basic questions:

1. Start with the why. Why do you need a campaign? What are its objectives?

2. What messages do you want to convey?

3. Who is your audience? Who do you need to reach?

4. Where does your audience spend most of its time? Which channels will you use?

5. When will you run the campaign? What is the best timing for when your audience is most receptive?

6. How will you execute the campaign? Who needs to be involved?

Be clear on the answers to these questions before you start. Then consider who you want to reach. The more specific you are, the easier it will be to plan your campaign. When considering your target audience, have one ideal person in mind. This will help you craft a clear message that will resonate with them. Don't be afraid of focusing on one individual that you want to reach.

Identify how you will reach your audience. Research where your target audience hangs out. What channels do they use most – social media, traditional press, industry publications or events? As an organisation, you need to go wherever your audience spends the most time. Finally, decide on when you want to begin your campaign and what the right time is for sending out your messages. This may be industry-specific or according to your recruitment cycles.

It is vital to gather the right people together into a diverse multi-disciplinary team to work on your campaign. Someone from Recruitment will be a key member. They can inform you of vacancies. Someone from Marketing can craft messages. There will be others. It is essential not to rely entirely on the HR department.

Four stages of running a campaign

The **AIDA** communications model is a simple marketing tool I recommend to organisations to plan their campaigns. The four stages of the model are:

- **Awareness or attention**
- **Interest**
- **Desire**
- **Action**

Using the Women in Technology conferences I organised for the BBC as an example of each stage: we increased awareness of the organisation as a tech employer through social media, blogging, third parties who had their own social media presence, other organisations' websites and through our own careers website. We posted intriguing questions online and used images of people working at the BBC to increase attention in our event.

We created interest by being mindful about the messages that we sent out into the world. We crafted these carefully so that they resonated with the people who were interested in working for us and wanted to know more. We also made short videos and articles about working at the Corporation.

We created desire in these people by building relationships with them so that they became even more interested. We answered their questions and posts on social media so that they saw the BBC as a truly responsive employer. We made the organisation a desirable place to want to work, which meant that they were eager to come to our events.

Finally, we gave every opportunity for people to take action. We created a clear, concise, and bold call to action which encouraged potential applicants to take the next step to apply. In your organisation it could be a button on your website that says 'Click here to apply to work for us' or 'Click here to sign up to our next event'. The clearer and the bolder your call to action, the more successful you will be.

Inclusive communications

As you create your campaign and given that this book is about diversity and inclusion, it is vital that your communications are inclusive too. All digital assets that you create have to be accessible. If you put an image online, make sure the image has 'alt' text, which is a description of the image that can be picked up by blind people using screen readers. PDF documents also need to be made accessible to screen readers. I am not an expert on this, but I recommend that you visit the Hassell Inclusion website to find out more. You will find the link in the Reference section at the back of this book. Websites also need to be accessible, as well as the images that you put up on social media. These platforms make it easy for you to add a description about the image which makes it accessible. Remember too that images should, in themselves, show the diversity of your organisation. Not everyone looks the same so avoid photographs that are not representative of the range of people working in your organisation.

Double-check the accessibility of venues. If you're going to hold an event, make sure that it's held in a venue with wheelchair access. A diversity and inclusion masterclass was being organised by an HR expert recently, which I really wanted to attend. But when I applied, I discovered that it was to be held in a venue that was not wheelchair accessible. I suggested to them that as it was a diversity and inclusion event, it was a poor show that they had immediately excluded wheelchair users by choosing this venue. Their response, at first, was that I wait and attend their workshop the following year. It was not without a lot of pressure from me that they eventually changed the venue to accommodate wheelchair users. How can an organisation claim to be inclusive when it takes an approach such as this?

The Power of Stories

If there is one thing that really does help promote you as an inclusive employer, it is storytelling. Stories have a huge impact in making your message land with impact. Telling a story about an individual in your organisation will make it easier for your potential employees to understand the culture of your organisation. Use a typical story structure – a beginning, middle and ending, elaborating on the person's struggle and lead the reader to the eventual outcome. People will absorb your organisation's message more easily through the telling of a story. It humanises the organisation and brings a lived experience to life, so that the reader can empathise with that individual and put themselves in their shoes. We know, through unconscious bias, that we are attracted to people like ourselves, that we have a similarity bias or in-group and out-group biases. Therefore, readers will relate to employees in your organisation.

Using storytelling to its maximum impact is about choosing the right people, empowering and supporting them to get their message out to the right people, and there are key steps you will need to take to ensure this strategy is fully effective.

- Firstly, allow your employees to tell their stories

- Empower them to write blogs and post them on your website or public sites like LinkedIn articles or Medium.com

- Empower them to talk openly on social media about what it is like to work for your organisation

- Give them the tools to write stories with impact

- Give your employees permission and freedom to speak about your organisation at conferences and events

- Identify the key people of influence in your organisation and empower them to promote your employer brand

- Give them a toolkit on your organisation's position on diversity and inclusion

- Educate your employees on the dos and don'ts of talking publicly about the organisation

- Interact on social media to give your organisation personality

- Trust your employees to reflect your organisation in the appropriate way

CASE STUDY: EY

'Be a strong disruptive voice in the market.'
— Sally Bucknell, Director of Diversity and
Inclusiveness at EY, UK

In recent years EY has increased its profile as an inclusive employer. Sally explains how EY achieved this. 'Like a lot of organisations, we went on a journey with this aspect of building the brand. To do this, you have to be prepared to run with some tension between how you would promote a brand to sell and how to convey the brand as who you are.'

Awards and Benchmarking

External recognition can be secured by gaining awards. However, Sally sounds a cautionary note on focusing on awards in isolation.

'It is a potentially dangerous game to play because it creates a perception which may or may not be matched by the reality. I call it the rhetoric reality gap. You have to be very careful and be robust as the diversity and inclusion leader when working out how beneficial these awards are.

The EY approach now is to be a strong disruptive voice in the market. We have chosen to steer clear of nearly all awards. We still choose to do some benchmarks if we genuinely believe they will give us some insights we wouldn't already have.'

Employee Experience

As EY does not rely on awards to build their profile as an inclusive employer, they have developed a two-strand approach that equips EY's people to tell their stories better.

One strand is using social media. EY asks people about their experience at the firm through networks or internal campaigns. EY asks questions like:

- When has diversity and inclusion been brought to life for you?

- What is your story?

- When did you feel you belong here?

- How do you feel EY is supporting and creating a sense of belonging for you?

EY creates short social media posts and stories from the answers. The firm also encourages people to tell their own stories and tag EY in. This type of social media activity creates an authentic voice.

Engaging Clients

The second approach is to equip client-facing employees to engage clients around diversity and inclusion from the outset. 'This supports our project team to add value to the solutions we create. We expect clients to welcome and embrace diversity and inclusion and that helps us create a sense of belonging across the project team. This leads to different conversations with clients.

These conversations might be with global organisations that already have diversity and inclusion strategies in place, but the impact hasn't always reached the factory floor. EY coming in connects the work to the ground level and clients know we mean business.'

Business Benefits

The evidence is that focusing on diversity and inclusion builds relationships and drives collaboration. 'Whilst it might seem like a soft subject for a client conversation it is one that creates trust. We are honest with clients; we work hard on this journey, but we are nowhere near there yet. Better relationships with clients mean that they buy more work from us.

Another tangible benefit is that an inclusive culture brings more talent to the firm. Diversity and inclusion is genuinely important to EY. Clients listen for this too. If they don't hear it, we won't win the business.'

Importance of Employee Lived Experience

Sally is clear about the importance of 'not telling tall stories or inconsistent stories around the business. Not everyone has the right experience all of the time. You can't always manage that, but you should have a mature response. We've steered away from a look how good we are message. You can create trouble for yourself if you hold yourself up as being universally good. The pain is doubly felt by people if the reality doesn't match up.'

The different internal networks have a valuable role to play. They mitigate against the rhetoric reality gap. They sense check what EY are saying about the culture and calibrate individual experiences. This allows the organisation to identify if an experience is an unfortunate event or if it is part of a deep cultural issue that the firm needs to address.

Making an Impact

Sally offers the following advice to businesses who want to make an impact on diversity and inclusion and are tempted to submit for awards or benchmarks, but might not have the capacity of a large organisation.

'Do not take a scattergun approach. Ask what you want to make progress on most and map that territory. Be clear about that focus first. Then map where the influencers are. Identify which are the bodies effectively driving change and get involved with them.'

Sally concludes, 'Focus on what you are trying to achieve. Work with the people and organisations who are change-making around your focus and your brand will benefit.'

In this chapter we have covered Celebrate – the final step of my Inclusive Growth System. My key message for this step is that a planned approach is vital to any successful celebration. Organisations tend to get seduced by glitzy, short-term things like winning awards. They end up wasting time filling out award entries that will never have a real impact on their organisation's profile. Every hour spent form-filling award entries is one hour less implementing the other six stages of my model outlined in Chapters One to Six: the ones that actually make the difference. Until you are clear about the culture you want for your organisation, you will send out the wrong message to the wrong target audience. Do the groundwork first – structure your thinking, organise your thoughts and only then can you create a compelling message that will truly demonstrate the diversity and inclusiveness of your organisation.

REFLECTION

Are you tempted to submit for lots of awards and benchmarks? Complete Chapters One to Six of my Inclusive Growth System so that you can be more strategic in raising your profile and celebrating your organisation as an inclusive employer.

1. What are the best mediums for your organisation to reach your intended audience, and what would go into your campaign plan?

2. What stories do you want to get out into the world?

3. How will you ensure that your communications, including digital channels, are inclusive and accessible?

Summary

The Inclusive Growth System is a tool that can result in better decision-making, greater innovation, better financial performance and higher employee retention. Simply by creating a workplace where people enjoy spending their time, feel that they can do their best work and make the best contributions possible, they are less likely to want to leave. Implementing this model gives a systematic framework to achieve these results in a sustainable way and enables you to future proof your organisation.

Let's just remind ourselves of the seven 'C's of the Inclusive Growth System:

- **Clarity**
- **Culture**
- **Change**
- **Colleague Experience and Design**
- **Cyber**
- **Collaboration**
- **Celebration**

Clarity   Culture   Change   Colleague Experience   Cyber   Collaboration   Celebration
& Design

The Inclusive Growth System

These seven steps will reduce the amount of time and money wasted on implementing 'box ticking' diversity and inclusion interventions piece meal and in silos.

You can now present your strategy to the Chief Executive of your organisation. Discuss what is the best way to implement diversity and inclusion and whether they will see faster results using the Inclusive Growth System. Get them to think about what growth represents for your organisation and how diversity and inclusion is an enabler of this growth. You might be a start-up. Diversity in your team will help you develop the best product possible for further investment. You could be a multinational organisation losing out on contracts because you are not sending diverse teams to pitch for new business. Or perhaps you are a not-for-profit organisation interested in growing your reputation.

When you have assessed your current situation and decided to make further improvements to your strategy, call me for expert advice, training or coaching on how to apply the Inclusive Growth System within your organisation.

References And Useful Resources

Agile Project Management, www.apm.org.uk
/resources/find-a-resource/agile-project-management

Bourke, J and Dillon, B (2016) 'The Six Signature
Traits of Inclusive Leadership', www2.deloitte.com
/us/en/insights/topics/talent/six-signature-traits-of
-inclusive-leadership.html

Brook, J (not dated) *Unpacking myths underpinning
the 9-Box Talent Grid*', www.strengthscope.com
/unpacking-myths-underpinning-9-box-talent-grid

Cave, A (Nov 2017) 'Culture Eats Strategy for
Breakfast. So What's for Lunch?' www.forbes.com
/sites/andrewcave/2017/11/09/culture-eats-strategy
-for-breakfast-so-whats-for-lunch/#2off6a867eof

Cook, J (2019) '"Racist" passport photo system
rejects image of a young black man despite meeting

government standards', *The Telegraph,* www.telegraph
.co.uk/technology/2019/09/19/racist-passport-photo
-system-rejects-image-young-black-man-despite

Down, R (Feb 2019) 'What is Company Culture and
Why is it Important?', www.breathehr.com/blog
/what-is-company-culture-and-why-is-it-important

Dragon Naturally Speaking, www.nuance.com
/dragon.html

Edgar Schein model of Organization Culture, www
.managementstudyguide.com/edgar-schein-model
.htm

Equality Act 2010, www.legislation.gov.uk/ukpga
/2010/15/contents

Gladkiy, S (Jun 2018) 'User-Centred Design: Process
and Benefits', https://uxplanet.org/user-centered
-design-process-and-benefits-fd9e431eb5a9

Greenwald, AG, McGhee, DE, Schwartz; Jordan, JLK
(1998) 'Measuring Individual Differences in Implicit
Cognition: The Implicit Association Test', *Journal of
Personality and Social Psychology,* 74(6), pp1464–1480

Groysberg, B, Lee, J, Price, J, and Cheng, J. Yo-Jud
(Jan–Feb 2018) 'The Leader's Guide to Corporate

Culture: How to manage the eight critical elements of organizational life.' *Harvard Business Review* 96, no. 1, p44–52

Hassell Inclusion www.hassellinclusion.com

Human Times http://human-times.com

Hunt V Prince S Dixon-Fyle S, Yee, L (Jan 2018) 'Delivering through Diversity' Report. McKinsey & Company, p8 www.mckinsey.com/business -functions/organization/our-insights/delivering -through-diversity-diversity_full-report.ashx

ISO 30071-1 Information technology – Development of user interface accessibility – Part 1: Code of practice for creating accessible ICT products and services, www.iso.org/standard/70913.html

JAWS, www.freedomscientific.com/products /software/jaws

Kotter, J 'Eight Step Process for Leading Change', www.kotterinc.com/8-steps-process-for-leading -change

McGregor-Smith, Baroness (Feb 2017) Race in the Workplace: The McGregor-Smith Review, www.gov .uk/government/publications/race-in-the-workplace -the-mcgregor-smith-review

Meetup application, www.Meetup.com

RACI Index, https://en.wikipedia.org/wiki
/Responsibility_assignment_matrix

Read & Write Gold, www.texthelp.com/en-gb
/products/read-write

Stonewall 'Safe Travels – Global Mobility for
LGBT Staff', www.equality.admin.cam.ac.uk/files
/stonewall_-_safe_travels_guide.pdf

Shaw Trust (part of the Disabled Living Foundation)
'*Key Facts*', www.dlf.org.uk/content/key-facts

Twine, France Winddance (2013) *Geographies of
Privilege*, Routledge, pp8–10

Weller, C (Apr 2019) 'The 5 Biggest Biases that Affect
Decision-Making', https://neuroleadership.com/your
-brain-at-work/seeds-model-biases-affect-decision
-making

W3C Accessibility Standards Overview www.w3.org
/WAI/standards-guidelines

Acknowledgements

To Chris, my boyfriend, for lovingly supporting me throughout the writing of this book, for listening to me as I ramble on about my ideas and for sharing his thoughts and opinions on the world with me.

To both of my parents who from a young age taught me that I did have a place in this world and that I could achieve anything I put my mind to.

To my clients for opening up their businesses to me and trusting me to support them in creating a more inclusive world. They have shared their own thoughts, ideas and opinions on how we can improve the future of work for everybody.

The Author

Toby Mildon is a Diversity and Inclusion Architect and founder of Mildon, a consultancy and advisory business. Toby works with businesses to re-engineer business processes and systems to minimise the impact of bias, to break down cultural barriers and to build a culture of inclusion.

Before setting up his consultancy, Toby worked for several years as a diversity and inclusion leader at Deloitte, and before that the BBC. He led countless initiatives to build diversity and culture in these big businesses, including targeted talent initiatives to get more women into tech, implement family-friendly policies and practices, and improve workplace accessibility to benefit all.

Toby's background is in tech and before specialising in diversity and inclusion he spent over a decade leading multinational projects in health tech, media and aviation. Contact Toby to continue the discussion:

✉ toby@mildon.co.uk
🌐 www.mildon.co.uk
in https://uk.linkedin.com/in/tobymildon

Printed in Great Britain
by Amazon